Microsoft®
Excel® 2013

Basic · Intermediate · **Advanced**

Microsoft®
Excel® 2013

Basic | Intermediate | **Advanced**

Lynn Wermers

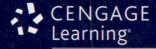

CENGAGE
Learning®

Australia • Brazil • Mexico • Singapore • United Kingdom • United States

Illustrated Course Guide: Microsoft® Excel® 2013 Advanced
Lynn Wermers

Senior Product Manger: Marjorie Hunt

Associate Product Manager: Amanda Lyons

Senior Content Developer: Christina Kling-Garrett

Content Developer: Megan Chrisman

Marketing Manager: Gretchen Swann

Developmental Editor: Barbara Clemens

Full-Service Project Management: GEX Publishing Services

Copyeditor: Kathy Orrino

Proofreader: Brandy Lilly

Indexer: Alexandra Nickerson

QA Manuscript Reviewers: John Freitas, Jeff Schwartz, Danielle Shaw, Susan Pedicini, Susan Whalen

Print Buyer: Fola Orekoya

Cover Designer: GEX Publishing Services

Cover Artist: © Katerina Havelkova/Shutterstock

Composition: GEX Publishing Services

For product information and technology assistance, contact us at **Cengage Learning Customer & Sales Support, 1-800-354-9706**

For permission to use material from this text or product, submit all requests online at **www.cengage.com/permissions**
Further permissions questions can be emailed to **permissionrequest@cengage.com**

Library of Congress Control Number: 2013953105
ISBN-13: 978-1-285-09341-3
ISBN-10: 1-285-09341-0

Cengage Learning
200 First Stamford Place, 4th Floor
Stamford, CT 06902
USA

Cengage Learning is a leading provider of customized learning solutions with office locations around the globe, including Singapore, the United Kingdom, Australia, Mexico, Brazil, and Japan. Locate your local office at: **www.cengage.com/global**

Cengage Learning products are represented in Canada by Nelson Education, Ltd.

For your course and learning solutions, visit **www.cengage.com**

Purchase any of our products at your local college store or at our preferred online store **www.cengagebrain.com**

Trademarks:
Some of the product names and company names used in this book have been used for identification purposes only and may be trademarks or registered trademarks of their respective manufacturers and sellers.

Microsoft and the Windows logo are registered trademarks of Microsoft Corporation in the United States and/or other countries. Cengage Learning is an independent entity from Microsoft Corporation, and not affiliated with Microsoft in any manner.

Printed in the United States of America
1 2 3 4 5 6 7 19 18 17 16 15 14

Brief Contents

Contents

Preface

Welcome to *Illustrated Course Guide: Microsoft Excel 2013 Advanced*. This book has a unique design: Each skill is presented on two facing pages, with steps on the left and screens on the right. The layout makes it easy to learn a skill without having to read a lot of text and flip pages to see an illustration.

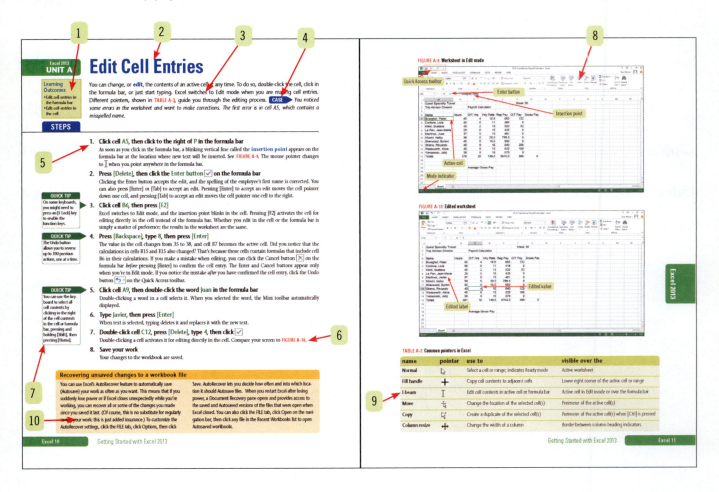

1. New! Learning Outcomes box lists measurable learning goals for which a student is accountable in that lesson.

2. Each two-page lesson focuses on a single skill.

3. Introduction briefly explains why the lesson skill is important.

4. A case scenario motivates the steps and puts learning in context.

5. Step-by-step instructions and brief explanations guide students through each hands-on lesson activity.

6. New! Figure references are now in red bold to help students refer back and forth between the steps and screenshots.

7. Tips and troubleshooting advice, right where you need it—next to the step itself.

8. New! Larger screenshots with green callouts keep students on track as they complete steps.

9. Tables provide summaries of helpful information such as button references or keyboard shortcuts.

10. Clues to Use yellow boxes provide useful information related to the lesson skill.

This book is an ideal learning tool for a wide range of learners—the "rookies" will find the clean design easy to follow and focused with only essential information presented, and the "hotshots" will appreciate being able to move quickly through the lessons to find the information they need without reading a lot of text. The design also makes this a great reference after the course is over! See the illustration on the left to learn more about the pedagogical and design elements of a typical lesson.

What's New in this Edition

- **Coverage** — Coverage of Excel 2013 helps students master advanced skills including using PivotTables, automating worksheet tasks using macros, programming with Excel, and more.

- **New! Learning Outcomes** — Each lesson displays a green Learning Outcomes box that lists skills-based or knowledge-based learning goals for which students are accountable. Each Learning Outcome maps to a variety of learning activities and assessments. (See the *New! Learning Outcomes* section on page xiii for more information.)

- **New! Updated Design** — This edition features many new design improvements to engage students — including larger lesson screenshots with green callouts placed on top, and a refreshed Unit Opener page.

- **New! Independent Challenge 4: Explore** — This new case-based assessment activity allows students to explore new skills and use creativity to solve a problem or create a project.

Assignments

This book includes a wide variety of high quality assignments you can use for practice and assessment. Assignments include:

- **Concepts Review** — Multiple choice, matching, and screen identification questions.

- **Skills Review** — Step-by-step, hands-on review of every skill covered in the unit.

- **Independent Challenges 1–3** — Case projects requiring critical thinking and application of the unit skills. The Independent Challenges increase in difficulty. The first one in each unit provides the most hand-holding; the subsequent ones provide less guidance and require more critical thinking and independent problem solving.

- **Independent Challenge 4: Explore** — Case projects that let students explore new skills that are related to the core skills covered in the unit and are often more open ended, allowing students to use creativity to complete the assignment.

- **Visual Workshop** — Critical thinking exercises that require students to create a project by looking at a completed solution; they must apply the skills they've learned in the unit and use critical thinking skills to create the project from scratch.

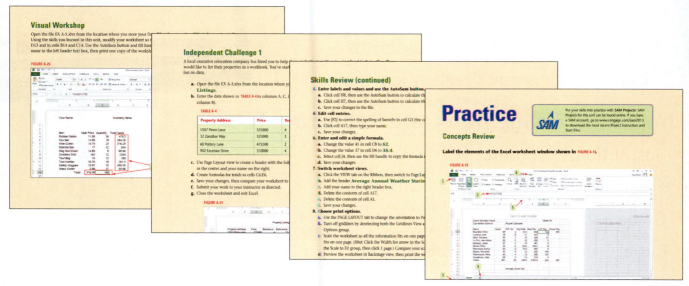

WHAT'S NEW FOR SAM 2013?

Get your students workplace ready with  **SAM**

The market-leading assessment and training solution for Microsoft Office

SAM 2013

Exciting New Features and Content

➤ Computer Concepts Trainings and Assessments *(shown on monitor)*

➤ Student Assignment Calendar

➤ All New SAM Projects

➤ Mac Hints

➤ More MindTap Readers

More Efficient Course Setup and Management Tools

➤ Individual Assignment Tool

➤ Video Playback of Student Clickpaths

➤ Express Assignment Creation Tool

Improved Grade Book and Reporting Tools

➤ Institutional Reporting

➤ Frequency Analysis Report

➤ Grade Book Enhancements

➤ Partial Credit Grading for Projects

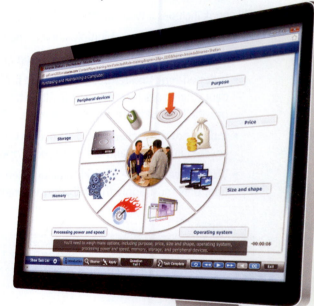

SAM is sold separately.

New! Learning Outcomes

Every 2-page lesson in this book now contains a green **Learning Outcomes box** that states the learning goals for that lesson.

- **What is a learning outcome?** A learning outcome states what a student is expected to know or be able to do after completing a lesson. Each learning outcome is skills-based or knowledge-based and is *measurable*. Learning outcomes map to learning activities and assessments.

- **How do students benefit from learning outcomes?** Learning outcomes tell students exactly what skills and knowledge they are *accountable* for learning in that lesson. This helps students study more efficiently and effectively and makes them more active learners.

- **How do instructors benefit from learning outcomes?** Learning outcomes provide clear, measurable, skills-based learning goals that map to various high-quality learning activities and assessments. A **Learning Outcomes Map**, available for each unit in this book, maps every learning outcome to the learning activities and assessments shown below.

Learning Outcomes Map to These Learning Activities:

1. **Book lessons:** Step-by-step tutorial on one skill presented in a two-page learning format
2. **SAM Training:** Short animations and hands-on practice activities in simulated environment *(SAM is sold separately.)*

Learning Outcomes Map to These Assessments:

1. **End-of-Unit Exercises: Concepts Review** (screen identification, matching, multiple choice); **Skills Review** (hands-on review of each lesson); **Independent Challenges** (hands-on, case-based review of specific skills); **Visual Workshop** (activity that requires student to build a project by looking at a picture of the final solution).
2. **Exam View Test Banks:** Objective-based questions you can use for online or paper testing.
3. **SAM Assessment:** Performance-based assessment in a simulated environment. *(SAM is sold separately.)*
4. **SAM Projects:** Auto-graded projects for Word, Excel, Access, and PowerPoint that students create. *(SAM is sold separately.)*
5. **Extra Independent Challenges:** Extra case-based exercises available in the Instructor Resources that cover various skills.

Learning Outcomes Map

A **Learning Outcomes Map**, contained in the Instructor Resources, provides a listing of learning activities and assessments for each learning outcome in the book.

Learning Outcomes Map
Microsoft Excel 2013 Illustrated Complete
Unit G

KEY:
IC=Independent Challenge   EIC=Extra Independent Challenge
VW=Visual Workshop

	Concepts Review	Skills Review	IC1	IC2	IC3	IC4	VW	EIC 1	EIC 2	Test Bank	SAM Assessment	SAM Projects	SAM Training
Plan a table													
Plan the data organization for a table	✓			✓						✓			
Plan the data elements for a table	✓			✓						✓			
Create and format a table													
Create a table		✓	✓	✓	✓	✓	✓			✓		✓	
Format a table		✓	✓	✓	✓	✓	✓			✓	✓	✓	✓
Add table data													
Add fields to a table		✓		✓	✓					✓	✓		✓
Add records to a table		✓		✓	✓					✓	✓		✓
Find and replace table data													
Find data in a table		✓	✓							✓	✓	✓	✓
Replace data in a table		✓	✓		✓					✓	✓	✓	✓
Delete table data													
Delete a table field		✓			✓					✓			
Delete a table row		✓			✓					✓	✓		✓
Remove duplicate data from a table		✓	✓										
Sort table data													
Sort a table in as...				✓									

Instructor Resources

This book comes with a wide array of high-quality technology-based, teaching tools to help you teach and to help students learn. The following teaching tools are available for download at our Instructor Companion Site. Simply search for this text at *login.cengage.com*. An instructor login is required.

- **New! Learning Outcomes Map** — A detailed grid for each unit (in Excel format) shows the learning activities and assessments that map to each learning outcome in that unit.

- **Instructor's Manual** — Available as an electronic file, the Instructor's Manual includes lecture notes with teaching tips for each unit.

- **Sample Syllabus** — Prepare and customize your course easily using this sample course outline.

- **PowerPoint Presentations** — Each unit has a corresponding PowerPoint presentation covering the skills and topics in that unit that you can use in lectures, distribute to your students, or customize to suit your course.

- **Figure Files** — The figures in the text are provided on the Instructor Resources site to help you illustrate key topics or concepts. You can use these to create your own slide shows or learning tools.

- **Solution Files** — Solution Files are files that contain the finished project that students create or modify in the lessons or end-of-unit material.

- **Solutions Document** — This document outlines the solutions for the end-of-unit Concepts Review, Skills Review, Independent Challenges and Visual Workshops. An Annotated Solution File and Grading Rubric accompany each file and can be used together for efficient grading.

- **ExamView Test Banks** — ExamView is a powerful testing software package that allows you to create and administer printed, computer (LAN-based), and Internet exams. Our ExamView test banks include questions that correspond to the skills and concepts covered in this text, enabling students to generate detailed study guides that include page references for further review. The computer-based and Internet testing components allow students to take exams at their computers, and also save you time by grading each exam automatically.

Key Facts About Using This Book

Data Files are needed: To complete many of the lessons and end-of-unit assignments, students need to start from partially completed Data Files, which help students learn more efficiently. By starting out with a Data File, students can focus on performing specific tasks without having to create a file from scratch. All Data Files are available as part of the Instructor Resources. Students can also download Data Files themselves for free at cengagebrain.com. (For detailed instructions, go to www.cengage.com/ct/studentdownload.)

System requirements: This book was developed using Microsoft Office 2013 Professional running on Windows 8. Note that Windows 8 is not a requirement for the units on Microsoft Office; Office 2013 runs virtually the same on Windows 7 and Windows 8. Please see Important Notes for Windows 7 Users on the next page for more information.

Screen resolution: This book was written and tested on computers with monitors set at a resolution of 1366 x 768. If your screen shows more or less information than the figures in this book, your monitor is probably set at a higher or lower resolution. If you don't see something on your screen, you might have to scroll down or up to see the object identified in the figure.

Tell Us What You Think!

We want to hear from you! Please email your questions, comments, and suggestions to the Illustrated Series team at: **illustratedseries@cengage.com**

Important Notes for Windows 7 Users

The screenshots in this book show Microsoft Office 2013 running on Windows 8. However, if you are using Microsoft Windows 7, you can still use this book because Office 2013 runs virtually the same on both platforms. There are only two differences that you will encounter if you are using Windows 7. Read this section to understand the differences.

Dialog boxes

If you are a Windows 7 user, dialog boxes shown in this book will look slightly different than what you see on your screen. Dialog boxes for Windows 7 have a light blue title bar, instead of a medium blue title bar. However, beyond this superficial difference in appearance, the options in the dialog boxes across platforms are the same. For instance, the screen shots below show the Font dialog box running on Windows 7 and the Font dialog box running on Windows 8.

FIGURE 1: Font dialog box in Windows 7

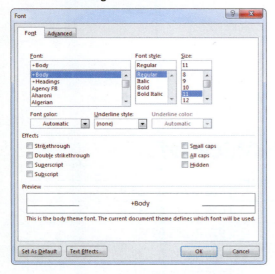

FIGURE 2: Font dialog box in Windows 8

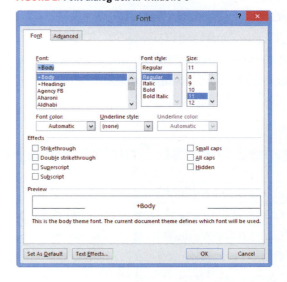

Alternate Steps for Starting an App in Windows 7

Nearly all of the steps in this book work exactly the same for Windows 7 users. However, starting an app (or program/application) requires different steps for Windows 7. The steps below show the Windows 7 steps for starting an app. (Note: Windows 7 alternate steps also appear in red Trouble boxes next to any step in the book that requires starting an app.)

Starting an app (or program/application) using Windows 7

1. Click the **Start button** on the taskbar to open the Start menu.
2. Click **All Programs**, then click the **Microsoft Office 2013 folder**. See Figure 3.
3. Click the app you want to use (such as **Excel 2013**).

FIGURE 3: Starting an app using Windows 7

Acknowledgements

Author Acknowledgements

Thanks to Barbara Clemens for her insightful contributions, invaluable feedback, great humor, and patience. Thanks also to Christina Kling-Garrett for her encouragement and support in guiding and managing this project.

–Lynn Wermers

Advisory Board Acknowledgements

We thank our Illustrated Advisory Board who gave us their opinions and guided our decisions as we developed all of the new editions for Microsoft Office 2013.

Merlin Amirtharaj, Stanly Community College

Londo Andrews, J. Sargeant Reynolds Community College

Rachelle Hall, Glendale Community College

Terri Helfand, Chaffey Community College

Sheryl Lenhart, Terra Community College

Dr. Jose Nieves, Lord Fairfax Community College

Illustrated Course Guides for Microsoft Office 2013

Illustrated Course Guide: Microsoft Word 2013 Basic	978-1-285-09336-9
Illustrated Course Guide: Microsoft Word 2013 Intermediate	978-1-285-09337-6
Illustrated Course Guide: Microsoft Word 2013 Advanced	978-1-285-09338-3
Illustrated Course Guide: Microsoft Excel 2013 Basic	978-1-285-09339-0
Illustrated Course Guide: Microsoft Excel 2013 Intermediate	978-1-285-09340-6
Illustrated Course Guide: Microsoft Excel 2013 Advanced	978-1-285-09341-3
Illustrated Course Guide: Microsoft Access 2013 Basic	978-1-285-09342-0
Illustrated Course Guide: Microsoft Access 2013 Intermediate	978-1-285-09343-7
Illustrated Course Guide: Microsoft Access 2013 Advanced	978-1-285-09344-4
Illustrated Course Guide: Microsoft PowerPoint 2013 Basic	978-1-285-09345-1
Illustrated Course Guide: Microsoft PowerPoint 2013 Advanced	978-1-285-09346-8

Analyzing Data with PivotTables

CASE ▶ Quest uses PivotTables to analyze sales data. Kate Morgan is preparing for the annual meeting for the United States region and asks you to analyze product sales in Quest's branches over the past year. You will create a PivotTable to summarize the 2016 sales data by quarter, product, and branch and illustrate the information using a PivotChart.

Unit Objectives

After completing this unit, you will be able to:

- Plan and design a PivotTable report
- Create a PivotTable report
- Change a PivotTable's summary function and design
- Filter and sort PivotTable data
- Update a PivotTable report
- Explore PivotTable Data Relationships
- Create a PivotChart report
- Use the GETPIVOTDATA function

Files You Will Need

EX L-1.xlsx   EX L-5.xlsx
EX L-2.xlsx   EX L-6.xlsx
EX L-3.xlsx   EX L-7.xlsx
EX L-4.xlsx

Plan and Design a PivotTable Report

Learning
Outcomes
• Develop guidelines
for a PivotTable
• Develop an
understanding of
PivotTable
vocabulary

The Excel **PivotTable Report** feature lets you summarize large amounts of columnar worksheet data in a compact table format. Then you can freely rearrange, or "pivot", PivotTable rows and columns to explore the relationships within your data by category. Creating a PivotTable report (often called a PivotTable) involves only a few steps. Before you begin, however, you need to review the data and consider how a PivotTable can best summarize it. **CASE** *Kate asks you to design a PivotTable to display Quest's sales information for its branches in the United States. You begin by reviewing guidelines for creating PivotTables.*

DETAILS

Before you create a PivotTable, think about the following guidelines:

• **Review the source data**

Before you can effectively summarize data in a PivotTable, you need to understand the source data's scope and structure. The source data does not have to be defined as a table, but should be in a table-like format. That is, it should have column headings, should not have any blank rows or columns, and should have the same type of data in each column. To create a meaningful PivotTable, make sure that one or more of the fields has repeated information so that the PivotTable can effectively group it. Also be sure to include numeric data that the PivotTable can total for each group. The data columns represent categories of data, which are called **fields**, just as in a table. You are working with sales information that Kate received from Quest's U.S. branch managers, shown in **FIGURE L-1**. Information is repeated in the Product ID, Category, Branch, and Quarter columns, and numeric information is displayed in the Sales column, so you will be able to summarize this data effectively in a PivotTable.

• **Determine the purpose of the PivotTable and write the names of the fields you want to include**

The purpose of your PivotTable is to summarize sales information by quarter across various branches. You want your PivotTable to summarize the data in the Product ID, Category, Branch, Quarter, and Sales columns, so you include those fields in your PivotTable.

• **Determine which field contains the data you want to summarize and which summary function you want to use**

You want to summarize sales information by summing the Sales field for each product in a branch by quarter. You'll do this by using the Excel SUM function.

• **Decide how you want to arrange the data**

The PivotTable layout you choose is crucial to delivering the message you intend. Product ID values will appear in the PivotTable columns, Branch and Quarter numbers will appear in rows, and the PivotTable will summarize Sales figures, as shown in **FIGURE L-2**.

• **Determine the location of the PivotTable**

You can place a PivotTable in any worksheet of any workbook. Placing a PivotTable on a separate worksheet makes it easier to locate and prevents you from accidentally overwriting parts of an existing sheet. You decide to create the PivotTable as a new worksheet in the current workbook.

FIGURE L-1: Sales worksheet

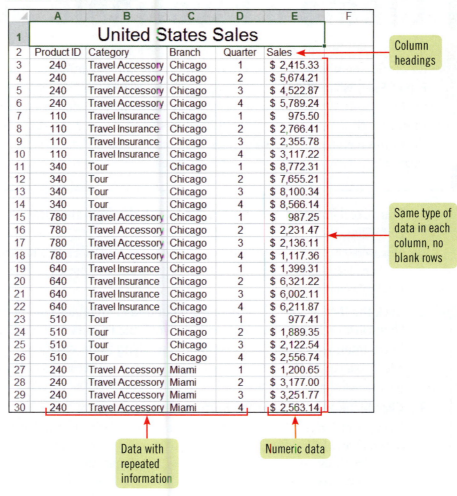

	A	B	C	D	E	F
1		United States Sales				
2	Product ID	Category	Branch	Quarter	Sales	
3	240	Travel Accessory	Chicago	1	$ 2,415.33	
4	240	Travel Accessory	Chicago	2	$ 5,674.21	
5	240	Travel Accessory	Chicago	3	$ 4,522.87	
6	240	Travel Accessory	Chicago	4	$ 5,789.24	
7	110	Travel Insurance	Chicago	1	$ 975.50	
8	110	Travel Insurance	Chicago	2	$ 2,766.41	
9	110	Travel Insurance	Chicago	3	$ 2,355.78	
10	110	Travel Insurance	Chicago	4	$ 3,117.22	
11	340	Tour	Chicago	1	$ 8,772.31	
12	340	Tour	Chicago	2	$ 7,655.21	
13	340	Tour	Chicago	3	$ 8,100.34	
14	340	Tour	Chicago	4	$ 8,566.14	
15	780	Travel Accessory	Chicago	1	$ 987.25	
16	780	Travel Accessory	Chicago	2	$ 2,231.47	
17	780	Travel Accessory	Chicago	3	$ 2,136.11	
18	780	Travel Accessory	Chicago	4	$ 1,117.36	
19	640	Travel Insurance	Chicago	1	$ 1,399.31	
20	640	Travel Insurance	Chicago	2	$ 6,321.22	
21	640	Travel Insurance	Chicago	3	$ 6,002.11	
22	640	Travel Insurance	Chicago	4	$ 6,211.87	
23	510	Tour	Chicago	1	$ 977.41	
24	510	Tour	Chicago	2	$ 1,889.35	
25	510	Tour	Chicago	3	$ 2,122.54	
26	510	Tour	Chicago	4	$ 2,556.74	
27	240	Travel Accessory	Miami	1	$ 1,200.65	
28	240	Travel Accessory	Miami	2	$ 3,177.00	
29	240	Travel Accessory	Miami	3	$ 3,251.77	
30	240	Travel Accessory	Miami	4	$ 2,563.14	

Column headings

Same type of data in each column, no blank rows

Data with repeated information

Numeric data

FIGURE L-2: PivotTable report based on Sales worksheet

Product ID values are column labels

	A	B	C	D	E	F	G	H	I	J
1										
2										
3										
4	Sum of Sales									
5		110	240	340	510	640	780	Grand Total		
6	Miami	$31,883.87	$10,192.56	$32,350.46	$9,567.18	$10,106.56	$10,001.51	$104,102.14		
7	1	$6,634.43	$1,200.65	$7,790.34	$2,310.34	$1,376.34	$1,766.34	$21,078.44		
8	2	$8,100.14	$3,177.00	$6,700.15	$2,524.87	$3,394.21	$3,524.21	$27,420.58		
9	3	$8,324.65	$3,251.77	$8,883.54	$2,183.54	$2,412.58	$2,307.53	$27,363.61		
10	4	$8,824.65	$2,563.14	$8,976.43	$2,548.43	$2,923.43	$2,403.43	$28,239.51		
11	New York	$15,057.69	$10,223.91	$29,818.65	$20,039.58	$8,856.97	$16,683.64	$100,680.44		
12	1	$4,921.45	$1,897.51	$6,258.21	$2,987.14	$1,305.47	$1,522.14	$18,891.92		
13	2	$3,319.92	$2,374.32	$7,628.78	$3,880.78	$2,183.98	$5,413.98	$24,801.76		
14	3	$4,176.89	$3,216.65	$8,198.90	$6,728.90	$2,577.98	$4,317.98	$29,217.30		
15	4	$2,639.43	$2,735.43	$7,732.76	$6,442.76	$2,789.54	$5,429.54	$27,769.46		
16	Chicago	$9,214.91	$18,401.65	$33,094.00	$7,546.04	$19,934.51	$6,472.19	$94,663.30		
17	1	$975.50	$2,415.33	$8,772.31	$977.41	$1,399.31	$987.25	$15,527.11		
18	2	$2,766.41	$5,674.21	$7,655.21	$1,889.35	$6,321.22	$2,231.47	$26,537.87		
19	3	$2,355.78	$4,522.87	$8,100.34	$2,122.54	$6,002.11	$2,136.11	$25,239.75		
20	4	$3,117.22	$5,789.24	$8,566.14	$2,556.74	$6,211.87	$1,117.36	$27,358.57		
21	Grand Total	$56,156.47	$38,818.12	$95,263.11	$37,152.80	$38,898.04	$33,157.34	$299,445.88		
22										
23										

PivotTable summarizes sales figures by product number, branch, and quarter

Branches and quarters are row labels

Create a PivotTable Report

Once you've planned and designed your PivotTable report, you can create it. After you create the PivotTable, you **populate** it by adding fields to areas in the PivotTable. A PivotTable has four areas: the Report Filter, which is the field by which you want to filter, or show selected data in, the PivotTable; the Row Labels, which contain the fields whose labels will describe the values in the rows; the Column Labels, which appear above the PivotTable values and describe the columns; and the Values, which summarize the numeric data. **CASE** *With the planning and design stage complete, you are ready to create a PivotTable that summarizes sales information.*

STEPS

1. **Start Excel if necessary, open the file EX L-1.xlsx from the location where you store your Data Files, then save it as EX L-US Sales**

   This worksheet contains the year's sales information for Quest's U.S. branches, including Product ID, Category, Branch, Quarter, and Sales. The records are sorted by branch. You decide to see what PivotTables Excel recommends for your data.

2. **Click the INSERT tab, click the Recommended PivotTables button in the Tables group, then click each of the recommended PivotTable layouts in the left side of the Recommended PivotTables dialog box, scrolling as necessary**

   The Recommended PivotTables dialog box opens, displaying recommended PivotTable layouts that summarize your data, as shown in **FIGURE L-3**. You decide to create your own PivotTable.

3. **Click Blank PivotTable at the bottom of the dialog box**

   A new, blank PivotTable appears on the left side of the worksheet and the PivotTable Fields List appears in a pane on the right, as shown in **FIGURE L-4**. You populate the PivotTable by clicking field check boxes in the PivotTable Fields List, often called the Field List. The diagram area at the bottom of the Field List represents the main PivotTable areas and helps you track field locations as you populate the PivotTable. You can also drag fields among the diagram areas to change the PivotTable layout.

4. **Click the Branch field check box in the Field List**

   Because the Branch field is a text, rather than a numeric field, Excel adds branch names to the rows area of the PivotTable, and adds the Branch field name to the ROWS area at the bottom of the Field List.

5. **Click the Product ID check box in the Field List**

   The Product ID information is automatically added to the PivotTable, and "Sum of Product ID" appears in the VALUES area in the diagram area. But because the data type of the Product ID field is numeric, the field is added to the VALUES area of the PivotTable and the Product ID values are summed, which is not meaningful. Instead, you want the Product IDs as column headers in the PivotTable.

6. **Click the Sum of Product ID list arrow in the VALUES area at the bottom of the PivotTable Fields List, then choose Move to Column Labels**

   The Product ID field becomes a column label, causing the Product ID values to appear in the PivotTable as column headers.

7. **Drag the Quarter field from the top of the PivotTable Fields List and drop it below the Branch field in the ROWS area at the bottom, select the Sales field check box in the PivotTable Fields List, then save the workbook**

   You have created a PivotTable that totals U.S. sales, with the Product IDs as column headers and Branches and Quarters as row labels. SUM is the Excel default function for data fields containing numbers, so Excel automatically calculates the sum of the sales in the PivotTable. The PivotTable tells you that Miami sales of Product #110 were twice the New York sales level and more than three times the Chicago sales level. Product #340 was the best selling product overall, as shown in the Grand Total row. See **FIGURE L-5**.

FIGURE L-3: Recommended PivotTables dialog box

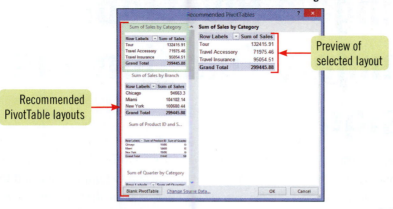

Recommended PivotTable layouts

Preview of selected layout

FIGURE L-4: Empty PivotTable ready to receive field data

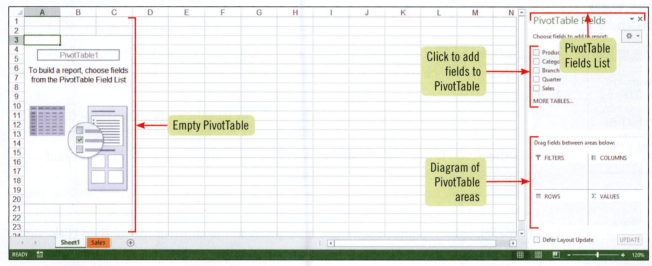

Click to add fields to PivotTable

PivotTable Fields List

Empty PivotTable

Diagram of PivotTable areas

FIGURE L-5: New PivotTable with fields in place

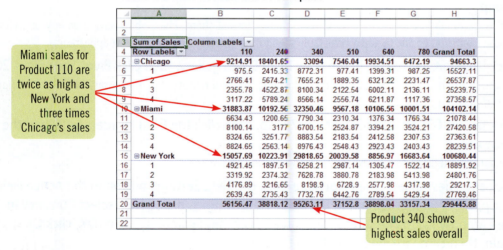

Miami sales for Product 110 are twice as high as New York and three times Chicago's sales

Product 340 shows highest sales overall

Changing the PivotTable layout

The default layout for PivotTables is the compact form; the row labels are displayed in a single column, and the second-level field items (such as the quarters in the U.S. Sales example) are indented for readability. You can change the layout of your PivotTable by clicking the PIVOTTABLE TOOLS DESIGN tab, clicking the Report Layout button in the Layout group, then clicking either Show in Outline Form or Show in Tabular Form. The tabular form and the outline form show each row label in its own column. The tabular and outline layouts take up more space on a worksheet than the compact layout.

Change a PivotTable's Summary Function and Design

A PivotTable's **summary function** controls what calculation Excel uses to summarize the table data. Unless you specify otherwise, Excel applies the SUM function to numeric data and the COUNT function to data fields containing text. However, you can easily change the default summary functions to different ones. **CASE** ▶ *Kate wants you to calculate the average sales for the U.S. branches using the AVERAGE function, and to improve the appearance of the PivotTable for her presentation.*

STEPS

1. **Right-click cell A3, then point to Summarize Values By in the shortcut menu**

   The shortcut menu shows that the Sum function is selected by default, as shown in **FIGURE L-6**.

2. **Click Average**

   The data area of the PivotTable shows the average sales for each product by branch and quarter, and cell A3 now contains "Average of Sales". You want to view the PivotTable data without the subtotals.

3. **Click the PIVOTTABLE TOOLS DESIGN tab, click the Subtotals button in the Layout group, then click Do Not Show Subtotals**

   After reviewing the data, you decide that it would be more useful to sum the sales information than to average it. You also want to redisplay the subtotals.

4. **Right-click cell A3, point to Summarize Values By in the shortcut menu, then click Sum**

   Excel recalculates the PivotTable—in this case, summing the sales data instead of averaging it.

5. **Click the Subtotals button in the Layout group, then click Show all Subtotals at Top of Group**

   Just as Excel tables have styles that let you quickly format them, PivotTables have a gallery of styles to choose from. You decide to add a PivotTable style to the PivotTable to improve its appearance.

6. **Click the More button ⏷ in the PivotTable Styles gallery, then click Pivot Style Light 20**

   To further improve the appearance of the PivotTable, you will remove the unnecessary headers of "Column Labels" and "Row Labels".

7. **Click the PIVOTTABLE TOOLS ANALYZE tab, then click the Field Headers button in the Show group**

   The data would be more readable if it were in currency format.

8. **Click any sales value in the PivotTable, click the Field Settings button in the Active Field group, click Number Format in the Value Field Settings dialog box, select Currency in the Category list, make sure Decimal places is 2 and Symbol is $, click OK, click OK again, then compare your PivotTable to FIGURE L-7**

   You decide to give the PivotTable sheet a more descriptive name. When you name a PivotTable sheet, it is best to avoid using spaces in the name. If a PivotTable name contains a space, you must put single quotes around the name if you refer to it in a function.

9. **Rename Sheet1 PivotTable, add your name to the worksheet footer, save the workbook, then preview the worksheet**

FIGURE L-6: Shortcut menu showing Sum function selected

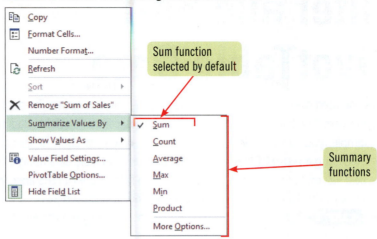

Sum function selected by default

Summary functions

FIGURE L-7: Formatted PivotTable

	A	B	C	D	E	F	G	H
1								
2								
3	**Sum of Sales**							
4		**110**	**240**	**340**	**510**	**640**	**780**	**Grand Total**
5	⊟**Chicago**	$9,214.91	$18,401.65	$33,094.00	$7,546.04	$19,934.51	$6,472.19	$94,663.30
6	1	$975.50	$2,415.33	$8,772.31	$977.41	$1,399.31	$987.25	$15,527.11
7	2	$2,766.41	$5,674.21	$7,655.21	$1,889.35	$6,321.22	$2,231.47	$26,537.87
8	3	$2,355.78	$4,522.87	$8,100.34	$2,122.54	$6,002.11	$2,136.11	$25,239.75
9	4	$3,117.22	$5,789.24	$8,566.14	$2,556.74	$6,211.87	$1,117.36	$27,358.57
10	⊟**Miami**	$31,883.87	$10,192.56	$32,350.46	$9,567.18	$10,106.56	$10,001.51	$104,102.14
11	1	$6,634.43	$1,200.65	$7,790.34	$2,310.34	$1,376.34	$1,766.34	$21,078.44
12	2	$8,100.14	$3,177.00	$6,700.15	$2,524.87	$3,394.21	$3,524.21	$27,420.58
13	3	$8,324.65	$3,251.77	$8,883.54	$2,183.54	$2,412.58	$2,307.53	$27,363.61
14	4	$8,824.65	$2,563.14	$8,976.43	$2,548.43	$2,923.43	$2,403.43	$28,239.51
15	⊟**New York**	$15,057.69	$10,223.91	$29,818.65	$20,039.58	$8,856.97	$16,683.64	$100,680.44
16	1	$4,921.45	$1,897.51	$6,258.21	$2,987.14	$1,305.47	$1,522.14	$18,891.92
17	2	$3,319.92	$2,374.32	$7,628.78	$3,880.78	$2,183.98	$5,413.98	$24,801.76
18	3	$4,176.89	$3,216.65	$8,198.90	$6,728.90	$2,577.98	$4,317.98	$29,217.30
19	4	$2,639.43	$2,735.43	$7,732.76	$6,442.76	$2,789.54	$5,429.54	$27,769.46
20	**Grand Total**	$56,156.47	$38,818.12	$95,263.11	$37,152.80	$38,898.04	$33,157.34	$299,445.88
21								
22								

Using the Show buttons

To display and hide PivotTable elements, you can use the buttons in the Show group on the PIVOTTABLE TOOLS ANALYZE tab. For example, the Field List button will hide or display the PivotTable Fields List. The +/– Buttons button will hide or display the Expand and Collapse Outline buttons, and the Field Headers button will hide or display the Row and Column Label headers on the PivotTable.

Learning
Outcomes
• Sort a PivotTable
using the fields
• Filter a PivotTable
using a slicer

Filter and Sort PivotTable Data

Just as you used filters to hide and display table data, you can restrict the display of PivotTable data. A **slicer** is a graphic object with a set of buttons that let you easily filter PivotTable data to show only the data you need. For example, you can use slicer buttons to show only data about a specific product. You can also filter a PivotTable using a **report filter**, which lets you filter PivotTable data using a list arrow to show data for one or more field values. For example, if you add a Month field to the FILTERS area, you can filter a PivotTable so that only January sales data appears in the PivotTable. You can also sort PivotTable data in ascending or descending order. **CASE** ▶ *Kate wants to see sales data about specific products for specific branches and quarters.*

STEPS

1. **Right-click cell H5, point to Sort in the shortcut menu, then click More Sort Options**
   The Sort By Value dialog box opens. As you select options in the dialog box, the Summary information at the bottom of the dialog box changes to describe the sort results using your field names.

2. **Click the Largest to Smallest option button to select it in the Sort options section, make sure the Top to Bottom option button is selected in the Sort direction section, review the sort description in the Summary section of the dialog box, then click OK**
   The branches appear in the PivotTable in decreasing order of total sales from top to bottom. You want to easily display the sales for specific product IDs at certain branches.

QUICK TIP
To select an external data source for a slicer, click a cell outside the PivotTable, click the INSERT tab, click the Slicer button in the Filters group, click the Show list arrow in the Existing Connections dialog box, choose a connection, click the connection you want to use, then click Open.

3. ▶ **Click any cell in the PivotTable, click the PIVOTTABLE TOOLS ANALYZE tab if necessary, click the Insert Slicer button in the Filter group, click the Product ID check box and the Branch check box in the Insert Slicers dialog box to select both fields, click OK, then drag the slicers to the right of the PivotTable**
   Slicers appear, with buttons representing the Product ID numbers and Branch names, as shown in **FIGURE L-8**. You want to filter the data to show only Product IDs 110 and 510 in the New York and Chicago branches.

4. **Click the 110 button in the Product ID slicer, press [CTRL] then click the 510 button in the Product ID slicer, release [CTRL], click the New York button in the Branch slicer, press [CTRL], click the Chicago button in the Branch slicer, then release [CTRL]**
   The PivotTable displays only the data for Product IDs 110 and 510 in New York and Chicago, as shown in **FIGURE L-9**. In the slicers, the Filter symbol changes, indicating the PivotTable is filtered to display the selected fields. You decide to clear the filter and remove the slicers.

5. **Click the Clear Filter button** ![clear filter icon] **in the Product ID slicer, click** ![clear filter icon] **in the Branch slicer, click the top of the Branch slicer, press [CTRL], click the top of the Product ID slicer, release [CTRL], right-click the Product ID slicer, then click Remove Slicers on the shortcut menu**
   You want to display the PivotTable data by quarter using a Report Filter.

TROUBLE
If the PivotTable Fields List is not visible, click the PIVOTTABLE TOOLS ANALYZE tab, and click the Field List button in the Show group.

6. ▶ **In the PivotTable Fields List, click the Quarter field list arrow in the ROWS area, then select Move to Report Filter**
   The Quarter field moves to cell A1, and a list arrow and the word "(All)" appear in cell B1. The list arrow lets you filter the data in the PivotTable by Quarter. "(All)" indicates that the PivotTable currently shows data for all quarters. You decide to filter the data to show only data for the fourth quarter.

QUICK TIP
You can add a slicer style, edit a slicer caption, and change the button order using the SLICER TOOLS OPTIONS tab.

7. ▶ **In the PivotTable cell B1, click the Quarter list arrow, click 4, click OK, then save your work**
   The PivotTable filters the sales data to display the fourth quarter only, as shown in **FIGURE L-10**. The Quarter field list arrow changes to a filter symbol. A filter symbol also appears to the right of the Quarter field in the PivotTable Fields List, indicating that the PivotTable is filtered and summarizes only a portion of the PivotTable data.

Analyzing Data with PivotTables

FIGURE L-8: Slicers for Product ID and Branch fields

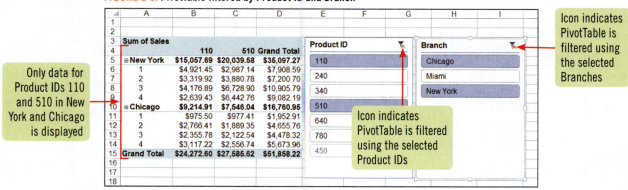

Click a Product ID to view its data

Click a Branch to view its data

FIGURE L-9: PivotTable filtered by Product ID and Branch

Only data for Product IDs 110 and 510 in New York and Chicago is displayed

Icon indicates PivotTable is filtered using the selected Branches

Icon indicates PivotTable is filtered using the selected Product IDs

	A	B	C	D	E	F	G	H	I
1									
2									
3	Sum of Sales				Product ID			Branch	
4		110	510	Grand Total					
5	New York	$15,057.69	$20,039.58	$35,097.27	110			Chicago	
6	1	$4,921.45	$2,987.14	$7,908.59	240			Miami	
7	2	$3,319.92	$3,880.78	$7,200.70	340			New York	
8	3	$4,176.89	$6,728.90	$10,905.79					
9	4	$2,639.43	$6,442.76	$9,082.19	510				
10	Chicago	$9,214.91	$7,546.04	$16,760.95	640				
11	1	$975.50	$977.41	$1,952.91	780				
12	2	$2,766.41	$1,889.35	$4,655.76					
13	3	$2,355.78	$2,122.54	$4,478.32	450				
14	4	$3,117.22	$2,556.74	$5,673.96					
15	Grand Total	$24,272.60	$27,585.62	$51,858.22					
16									
17									
18									

FIGURE L-10: PivotTable filtered by fourth quarter

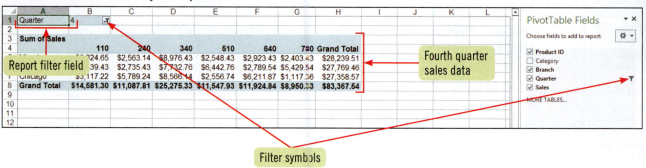

Report filter field

Fourth quarter sales data

Filter symbols

	A	B	C	D	E	F	G	H
1	Quarter	4						
2								
3	Sum of Sales							
4		110	240	340	510	640	780	Grand Total
5		$24.65	$2,563.14	$8,976.43	$2,548.43	$2,923.43	$2,403.43	$28,239.51
6		39.43	$2,735.43	$7,732.76	$6,442.76	$2,789.54	$5,429.54	$27,769.46
7	Chicago	$3,117.22	$5,789.24	$8,566.14	$2,556.74	$6,211.87	$1,117.36	$27,358.57
8	Grand Total	$14,581.30	$11,087.81	$25,275.33	$11,547.93	$11,924.84	$8,950.53	$83,367.64

PivotTable Fields

Choose fields to add to report:
- ☑ Product ID
- ☐ Category
- ☑ Branch
- ☑ Quarter
- ☑ Sales

MORE TABLES...

Filtering PivotTables using multiple values

You can select multiple values when filtering a PivotTable report using a report filter. After clicking a field's report filter list arrow in the top section of the PivotTable Fields List or in cell B1 on the PivotTable itself, click the Select Multiple Items check box at the bottom of the filter selections. This lets you select multiple values for the filter. For example, selecting 1 and 2 as the report filter in a PivotTable with quarters would display all of the data for the first two quarters. You can also select multiple values for the row and column labels by clicking the PIVOTTABLE TOOLS ANALYZE tab, clicking the Field Headers button in the Show group, clicking the Row Labels list arrow or the Column Labels list arrow in cells A4 and B3 on the PivotTable and selecting the data items that you want to display.

Update a PivotTable Report

**Learning
Outcomes**
• Add data to a
PivotTable data
source
• Refresh a PivotTable

The data in a PivotTable report looks like typical worksheet data. Because the PivotTable data is linked to a **data source** (the data you used to create the PivotTable), however, the values and results in the PivotTable are read-only values. That means you cannot move or modify a part of a PivotTable by inserting or deleting rows, editing results, or moving cells. To change PivotTable data, you must edit the items directly in the data source, then update, or **refresh**, the PivotTable to reflect the changes. **CASE** *Kate just learned that sales information for a custom group tour sold in New York during the fourth quarter was never entered into the Sales worksheet. Kate asks you to add information about this tour to the data source and PivotTable. You start by inserting a row for the new information in the Sales worksheet.*

STEPS

QUICK TIP

If you want to change the PivotTable's source data range, click the PIVOTTABLE TOOLS ANALYZE tab, then click the Change Data Source button in the Data group.

1. **Click the Sales sheet tab**

   By inserting the new row in the correct position by branch, you will not need to sort the data again.

2. **Scroll to and right-click the row 51 heading, then click Insert on the shortcut menu**

   A blank row appears as the new row 51, and the data in the old row 51, moves down to row 52. You now have room for the tour data.

3. **Enter the data for the new tour in row 51 using the following information**

Product ID	450
Category	Tour
Branch	New York
Quarter	4
Sales	3102.95

   The PivotTable does not yet reflect the additional data.

QUICK TIP

To remove a field from a PivotTable, click its check box to remove the check mark.

4. **Click the PivotTable sheet tab, then verify that the Quarter 4 data appears**

   The PivotTable does not currently include the new tour information, and the grand total is $83,367.54. Before you refresh the PivotTable data, you need to make sure that the cell pointer is located within the PivotTable range.

QUICK TIP

If you want Excel to refresh a PivotTable report automatically when you open a workbook, click the Options button in the PivotTable group, click the Data tab in the PivotTable Options dialog box, click the Refresh data when opening the file check box, then click OK.

5. **Click anywhere within the PivotTable if necessary, click the PIVOTTABLE TOOLS ANALYZE tab, then click the Refresh button in the Data group**

   The PivotTable now contains a column for the new product ID, which includes the new tour information, in column H, and the grand total has increased by the amount of the tour's sales ($3,102.95) to $86,470.49, as shown in **FIGURE L-11**.

6. **Save the workbook**

Grouping PivotTable data

You can group PivotTable data to analyze specific values in a field as a unit. For example, you may want to group sales data for quarters one and two to analyze sales for the first half of the year. To group PivotTable data, first select the rows and columns that you want to group, click the PIVOTTABLE TOOLS ANALYZE tab, then click the Group Selection button in the Group group. To summarize grouped data, click the Field Settings button in the Active Field group, click the Custom option button in the Field Settings dialog box, select the function that you want to use to summarize the data, then click OK. To collapse the group and show the function results, click the Collapse Outline button — next to the group name. You can click the Expand Outline button + next to the group name to display the rows or columns in the group. To ungroup data, select the Group name in the PivotTable, then click the Ungroup button in the Group group.

FIGURE L-11: Updated PivotTable report

New data is added

	A	B	C	D	E	F	G	H	I
1	Quarter	4							
2									
3	**Sum of Sales**								
4		110	240	340	510	640	780	450	**Grand Total**
5	New York	$2,639.43	$2,735.43	$7,732.76	$6,442.76	$2,789.54	$5,429.54	$3,102.95	$30,872.41
6	Miami	$8,824.65	$2,563.14	$8,976.43	$2,548.43	$2,923.43	$2,403.43		$28,239.51
7	Chicago	$3,117.22	$5,789.24	$8,566.14	$2,556.74	$6,211.87	$1,117.36		$27,358.57
8	**Grand Total**	$14,581.30	$11,087.81	$25,275.33	$11,547.93	$11,924.84	$8,950.33	$3,102.95	$86,470.49
9									
10									

Totals are updated to include the new data

Adding a calculated field to a PivotTable

You can use formulas to analyze PivotTable data in a field by adding a calculated field. A calculated field appears in the Field List and can be manipulated like other PivotTable fields. To add a calculated field, click any cell in the PivotTable, click the PIVOTTABLE TOOLS ANALYZE tab, click the Fields, Items, & Sets button in the Calculations group, then click Calculated Field. The Insert Calculated Field dialog box opens. Enter the field name in the Name text box, click in the Formula text box, click a field name in the Fields list that you want to use in the formula, and click Insert Field. Use standard arithmetic operators to enter the formula you want to use. For example **FIGURE L-12** shows a formula to increase Sales data by 10 percent. After entering the formula in the Insert Calculated Field dialog box, click Add, then click OK. The new field with the formula results appears in the PivotTable, and the field is added to the PivotTable Fields List as shown in **FIGURE L-13**.

FIGURE L-12: Insert Calculated Field dialog box

New field name

Formula to increase sales by 10%

Fields that can be used in the formula

Insert Calculated Field

Name: Increase Sales

Formula: = Sales*1.1

Add
Delete

Fields:
Product ID
Category
Branch
Quarter
Sales

Insert Field

OK   Close

FIGURE L-13: PivotTable with calculated field

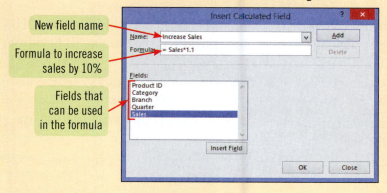

New calculated field

	A	B	C	D	E	F	G	H
1	Quarter	4						
2								
3		110		240		340		
4		Sum of Sales	Sum of Increase Sales	Sum of Sales	Sum of Increase Sales	Sum of Sales	Sum of Increase Sales	Sum of Sa
5	New York	$2,639.43	$ 2,903.37	$2,735.43	$ 3,008.97	$7,732.76	$ 8,506.04	$6,44
6	Miami	$8,824.65	$ 9,707.12	$2,563.14	$ 2,819.45	$8,976.43	$ 9,874.07	$2,54
7	Chicago	$3,117.22	$ 3,428.94	$5,789.24	$ 6,368.16	$8,566.14	$ 9,422.75	$2,55
8	Grand Total	$14,581.30	$ 16,039.43	$11,087.81	$ 12,196.59	$25,275.33	$ 27,802.86	$11,54
9								
10								
11								
12								

PivotTable Fields

Choose fields to add to report:

☑ Product ID
☐ Category
☑ Branch
☑ Quarter
☑ Sales
☑ Increase Sales

MORE TABLES...

Explore PivotTable Data Relationships

Learning Outcomes
• Change a PivotTable's organization
• Add fields to a PivotTable

What makes a PivotTable such a powerful analysis tool is the ability to change the way data is organized in the report. By moving fields to different positions in the report, you can explore relationships and trends that you might not see in the original report structure. **CASE** *Kate asks you to include category information in the sales report. She is also interested in viewing the PivotTable in different arrangements to find the best organization of data for her presentation.*

STEPS

1. **Make sure that the PivotTable sheet is active, that the active cell is located anywhere inside the PivotTable, and that the PivotTable Fields List is visible**

2. **Click the Category check box in the Field List**

   The category data is added to the ROWS area below the corresponding branch data. As you learned earlier, you can move fields within an area of a PivotTable by dragging and dropping them to the desired location.

3. **In the diagram section of the Field List, locate the ROWS area, then drag the Category field up and drop it above the Branch field**

   The category field is now the outer or upper field, and the branch field is the inner or lower field. The PivotTable is restructured to display the sales data by the category values and then the branch values within the category field. The subtotals now reflect the sum of the categories, as shown in **FIGURE L-14**. You can also move fields to new areas in the PivotTable.

4. **In the diagram area of the Field List, drag the Category field from the ROWS area to anywhere in the COLUMNS area, then drag the Product ID field from the COLUMNS area to the ROWS area below the Branch field**

   The PivotTable now displays the sales data with the category values in the columns and then the product IDs grouped by branches in the rows. The product ID values are indented below the branches because the Product ID field is the inner row label.

5. **In the diagram area of the Field List, drag the Category field from the COLUMNS area to the FILTERS area above the Quarter field, then drag the Product ID field from the ROWS area to the COLUMNS area**

   The PivotTable now has two report filters. The upper report filter, Category, summarizes data using all of the categories. Kate asks you to display the tour sales information for all quarters.

6. **Click the Category list arrow in cell B1 of the PivotTable, click Tour, click OK, click the Quarter filter list arrow in cell B2, click All, then click OK**

   The PivotTable displays sales totals for the Tour category for all quarters. Kate asks you to provide the sales information for all categories.

7. **Click the Category filter arrow, click All, then click OK**

   The completed PivotTable appears as shown in **FIGURE L-15**.

8. **Save the workbook, change the page orientation of the PivotTable sheet to Landscape, then preview the PivotTable**

FIGURE L-14: PivotTable structured by branches within categories

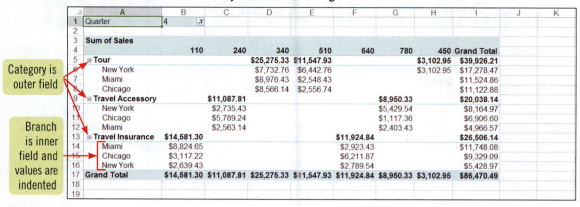

Category is outer field

Branch is inner field and values are indented

FIGURE L-15: Completed PivotTable report

	A	B	C	D	E	F	G	H	I
1	Category	(All)							
2	Quarter	(All)							
3									
4	Sum of Sales								
5		110	240	340	510	640	780	450	Grand Total
6	Miami	$31,883.87	$10,192.56	$32,350.46	$9,567.18	$10,106.56	$10,001.51		$104,102.14
7	New York	$15,057.69	$10,223.91	$29,818.65	$20,039.58	$8,856.97	$16,683.64	$3,102.95	$103,783.39
8	Chicago	$9,214.91	$18,401.65	$33,094.00	$7,546.04	$19,934.51	$6,472.19		$94,663.30
9	Grand Total	$56,156.47	$38,818.12	$95,263.11	$37,152.80	$38,898.04	$33,157.34	$3,102.95	$302,548.83
10									
11									

Adding conditional formatting to a PivotTable

You can add conditional formatting to a PivotTable to make it easier to compare the data values. The conditional formatting is applied to cells in a PivotTable the same way as it is to non-PivotTable data. The conditional formatting rules follow the PivotTable cells when you move fields to different areas of the PivotTable. **FIGURE L-16** shows a PivotTable that uses data bars to visually display the sales data.

FIGURE L-16: PivotTable with conditional formatting

	A	B	C	D	E	F	G	H	I	J
1	Category	(All)								
2	Quarter	(All)								
3										
4	Sum of Sales									
5		110	240	340	510	640	780	450	Grand Total	
6	Miami	$31,883.87	$10,192.56	$32,350.46	$9,567.18	$10,106.56	$10,001.51		$104,102.14	
7	New York	$15,057.69	$10,223.91	$29,818.65	$20,039.58	$8,856.97	$16,683.64	$3,102.95	$103,783.39	
8	Chicago	$9,214.91	$18,401.65	$33,094.00	$7,546.04	$19,934.51	$6,472.19		$94,663.30	
9	Grand Total	$56,156.47	$38,818.12	$95,263.11	$37,152.80	$38,898.04	$33,157.34	$3,102.95	$302,548.83	
10										
11										
12										

Excel 2013

Create a PivotChart Report

A **PivotChart report** is a chart that you create from data or from a PivotTable report. **TABLE L-1** describes how the elements in a PivotTable report correspond to the elements in a PivotChart report. When you create a PivotChart directly from data, Excel automatically creates a corresponding PivotTable report. If you change a PivotChart report by filtering or sorting the charted elements, Excel updates the corresponding PivotTable report to show the new data values. You can move the fields of a PivotChart using the PivotTable Fields List window; the new layout will be reflected in the PivotTable. **CASE** ▶ *Kate wants you to chart the fourth quarter tour sales and the yearly tour sales average for her presentation. You create the PivotChart report from the PivotTable data.*

STEPS

1. **Click the Category list arrow in cell B1, click Tour, click OK, click the Quarter list arrow, click 4, then click OK**

   The fourth quarter tour sales information appears in the PivotTable. You want to create the PivotChart from the PivotTable information you have displayed.

2. **Click any cell in the PivotTable, click the PIVOTTABLE TOOLS ANALYZE tab, then click the PivotChart button in the Tools group**

   The Insert Chart dialog box opens and shows a gallery of chart types.

3. **Click the Clustered Column chart if necessary, then click OK**

   The PivotChart appears on the worksheet as shown in **FIGURE L-17**. The chart has Field buttons that let you filter and sort a PivotChart in the same way you do a PivotTable. It will be easier to view the PivotChart if it is on its own sheet.

4. **Click the PIVOTCHART TOOLS DESIGN tab, click the Move Chart button in the Location group, click the New sheet option button, type PivotChart in the text box, click OK**

   The chart represents the fourth quarter tour sales. Kate asks you to change the chart to show the average sales for all quarters.

5. **Click the Quarter field button at the top of the PivotChart, click All, then click OK**

   The chart now represents the sum of tour sales for the year as shown in **FIGURE L-18**. You can change a PivotChart's summary function to display averages instead of totals.

6. **Click the Sum of Sales list arrow in the VALUES area of the PivotTable Fields List, click Value Field Settings, click Average on the Summarize Values By tab, then click OK**

   The PivotChart report recalculates to display averages. The chart would be easier to understand if it had a title.

7. **Click the PIVOTCHART TOOLS DESIGN tab, click the Add Chart Element button in the Chart Layouts group, point to Chart Title, click Above Chart, type Average Tour Sales, press [Enter], then drag the chart title border to center the title over the columns**

   You are finished filtering the chart data and decide to remove the field buttons.

8. **Click the PIVOTCHART TOOLS ANALYZE tab, then click the Field Buttons button in the Show/Hide group**

9. **Enter your name in the PivotChart sheet footer, save the workbook, then preview the PivotChart report**

   The final PivotChart report displaying the average tour sales for the year is shown in **FIGURE L-19**.

FIGURE L-17: PivotChart with fourth quarter tour sales

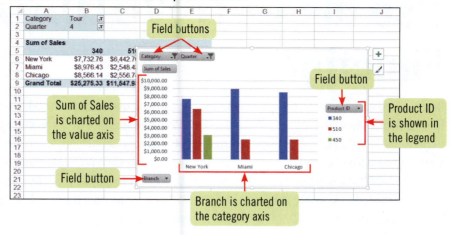

Field buttons

Field button

Product ID is shown in the legend

Sum of Sales is charted on the value axis

Field button

Branch is charted on the category axis

FIGURE L-18: PivotChart displaying tour sales for the year

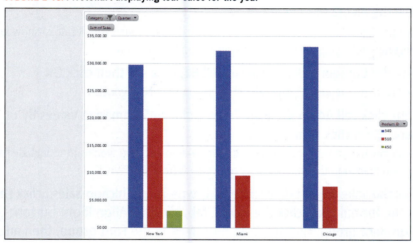

FIGURE L-19: Completed PivotChart report

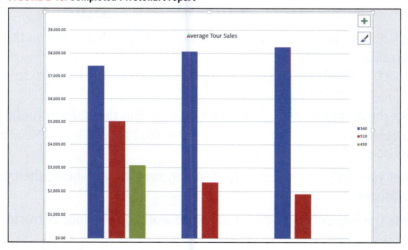

TABLE L-1: PivotTable and PivotChart elements

PivotTable items	PivotChart items
Row labels	Axis fields
Column labels	Legend fields
Report filters	Report filters

© 2014 Cengage Learning

Use the GETPIVOTDATA Function

Learning Outcomes
• Analyze the GETPIVOTDATA function
• Retrieve information from a PivotTable using the GETPIVOTDATA function

Because you can rearrange a PivotTable so easily, you can't use an ordinary cell reference when you want to reference a PivotTable cell in another worksheet. The reason is that if you change the way data is displayed in a PivotTable, the data moves, making an ordinary cell reference incorrect. Instead, to retrieve summary data from a PivotTable, you need to use the Excel GETPIVOTDATA function. See **FIGURE L-20** for the GETPIVOTDATA function format. **CASE** *Kate wants to include the yearly sales total for the Chicago branch in the Sales sheet. She asks you to retrieve this information from the PivotTable and place it in the Sales sheet. You use the GETPIVOTDATA function to retrieve this information.*

STEPS

1. **Click the PivotTable sheet tab**

   The sales figures in the PivotTable are average values for tours. You decide to show sales information for all categories and change the summary information back to Sum.

2. **Click the Category filter arrow in cell B1, click All, then click OK**

   The PivotChart report displays sales information for all categories.

3. **Right-click cell A4 on the PivotTable, point to Summarize Values By on the shortcut menu, then click Sum**

   The PivotChart report recalculates to display sales totals. Next, you want to include the total for sales for the Chicago branch in the Sales sheet by retrieving it from the PivotTable.

4. **Click the Sales sheet tab, click cell G1, type Total Chicago Sales:, click the Enter button ✓ on the formula bar, click the HOME tab, click the Align Right button ≡ in the Alignment group, click the Bold button B in the Font group, then adjust the width of column G to display the label in cell G1**

   You want the GETPIVOTDATA function to retrieve the total Chicago sales from the PivotTable. Cell I8 on the PivotTable contains the data you want to display on the Sales sheet.

5. **Click cell G2, type =, click the PivotTable sheet tab, click cell I8 on the PivotTable, then click ✓**

   The GETPIVOTDATA function, along with its arguments, is inserted into cell G2 of the Sales sheet, as shown in **FIGURE L-21**. You want to format the sales total.

6. **Click the Accounting Number Format button $ in the Number group**

   The current sales total for the Chicago branch is $94,663.30. This is the same value displayed in cell I8 of the PivotTable.

7. **Enter your name in the Sales sheet footer, save the workbook, then preview the Sales worksheet**

8. **Close the file, exit Excel, then submit the workbook to your instructor**

   The Sales worksheet is shown in **FIGURE L-22**.

FIGURE L-20: Format of GETPIVOTDATA function

GETPIVOTDATA("Sales",PivotTable!$A$4,"Branch","Chicago")

| Field where data is extracted from | PivotTable name and cell in the report that contains the data you want to retrieve | Field and value pair that describe the data you want to retrieve |

FIGURE L-21: GETPIVOTDATA function in the Sales sheet

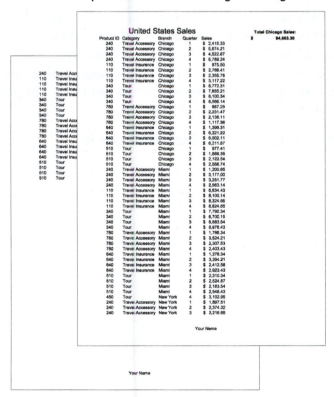

Function is entered into the formula bar and result appears in the cell

FIGURE L-22: Completed Sales worksheet showing total Chicago sales

Analyzing Data with PivotTables

Practice

Put your skills into practice with SAM! If you have a SAM account, go to www.cengage.com/sam2013 to access SAM assignments for this unit.

Concepts Review

FIGURE L-23

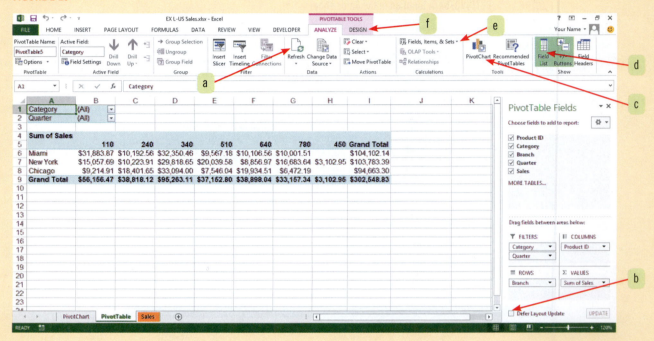

1. Which element do you click to create a calculated field in a PivotTable?
2. Which element do you click to create a chart based on the data in a PivotTable?
3. Which element do you click to display a gallery of PivotTable Styles?
4. Which element do you click to control when PivotTable changes will occur?
5. Which element do you click to display or hide the PivotTable Fields List pane?
6. Which element do you click to update a PivotTable?

Match each term with the statement that best describes it.

7. PivotTable Row Label   **a.** Retrieves information from a PivotTable

8. Slicer   **b.** Default layout for a PivotTable

9. Compact form   **c.** PivotTable filtering tool

10. Summary function   **d.** PivotChart axis field

11. GETPIVOTDATA function   **e.** Determines if data is summed or averaged

Select the best answer from the list of choices.

12. When a numeric field is added to a PivotTable, it is placed in the _____ area.
    a. VALUES
    b. ROWS
    c. COLUMNS
    d. FILTERS

13. Which PivotTable report area allows you to display only certain data using a list arrow?
    a. Values
    b. Column Labels
    c. Report Filter
    d. Row Labels

14. To make changes to PivotTable data, you must:
    a. Drag a column header to the column area.
    b. Create a page field.
    c. Edit cells in the PivotTable, then refresh the source list.
    d. Edit cells in the source list, then refresh the PivotTable.

15. When a nonnumeric field is added to a PivotTable, it is placed in the _____ area.
    a. VALUES
    b. Report Filter
    c. ROWS
    d. COLUMNS

Skills Review

1. **Plan and design a PivotTable report.**
    a. Start Excel, open the file titled EX L-2.xlsx from the location where you store your Data Files, then save it as **EX L-Product Sales**.
    b. Review the fields and data values in the worksheet.
    c. Verify that the worksheet data contains repeated values in one or more fields.
    d. Verify that there are not any blank rows or columns in the range A1:E25.
    e. Verify that the worksheet data contains a field that can be summed in a PivotTable.

2. **Create a PivotTable report.**
    a. Create a PivotTable report on a new worksheet using the Sales worksheet data in the range A1:E25.
    b. Add the Product ID field in the PivotTable Fields List pane to the COLUMNS area.
    c. Add the Sales field in the PivotTable Fields List pane to the VALUES Area.
    d. Add the Store field in the PivotTable Fields List pane to the ROWS area.
    e. Add the Sales Rep field in the PivotTable Fields List pane to the ROWS area below the Store field.

3. **Change a PivotTable's summary function and design.**
    a. Change the PivotTable summary function to Average.
    b. Rename the new sheet **Sales PivotTable**.
    c. Change the PivotTable Style to Pivot Style Light 20. Format the sales values in the PivotTable as Currency with a $ symbol and two decimal places.
    d. Enter your name in the center section of the PivotTable report footer, then save the workbook.
    e. Change the Summary function back to Sum. Remove the headers "Row Labels" and "Column Labels."

4. **Filter and sort PivotTable data.**
    a. Sort the stores in ascending order by total sales.
    b. Use slicers to filter the PivotTable to display sales for product IDs 100 and 200 in the DC and Seattle stores.
    c. Clear the filters and delete the slicers.
    d. Add the Region field to the FILTERS area in the PivotTable Fields List pane. Use the FILTERS list arrow to display sales for only the East region. Display sales for all regions.
    e. Save the workbook.

5. **Update a PivotTable report.**
    a. With the Sales PivotTable sheet active, note the NY total for Product ID 300.
    b. Activate the Sales sheet, and change K. Lyons's sales of Product ID 300 in cell D7 to **$9,000**.
    c. Refresh the PivotTable so it reflects the new sales figure.
    d. Verify the NY total for Product ID 300 decreased to $18,254. Save the workbook.

Skills Review (continued)

6. **Explore PivotTable Data Relationships.**

   a. In the PivotTable Fields List, drag the Product ID field from the COLUMNS area to the ROWS area below the Sales Rep field. Drag the Sales Rep field from the ROWS area to the COLUMNS area.

   b. Drag the Store field from the ROWS area to the FILTERS area below the Region field. Drag the Product ID field back to the COLUMNS area.

   c. Drag the Store field back to the ROWS area.

   d. Remove the Sales Rep field from the PivotTable.

   e. Compare your completed PivotTable to **FIGURE L-24**, save the workbook.

7. **Create a PivotChart report.**

   a. Use the existing PivotTable data to create a Clustered Column PivotChart report.

   b. Move the PivotChart to a new worksheet, and name the sheet **PivotChart**.

   c. Add the title **Total Sales** above the chart.

   d. Filter the chart to display only sales data for the east region. Display the sales data for all regions. Hide all of the Field Buttons.

   e. Add your name to the center section of the PivotChart sheet footer. Compare your PivotChart to **FIGURE L-25**, save the workbook.

8. **Use the GETPIVOTDATA function.**

   a. In cell D27 of the Sales sheet type =, click the Sales PivotTable sheet, click the cell that contains the grand total for LA, then press [Enter].

   b. Review the GETPIVOTDATA function that was entered in cell D27.

   c. Enter your name in the Sales sheet footer, compare your Sales sheet to **FIGURE L-26**, save the workbook, then preview the sales worksheet.

   d. Close the workbook and exit Excel. Submit the workbook to your instructor.

Independent Challenge 1

You are the accountant for the Service Department of an HVAC company. The Service Department employs three technicians that service heating and air conditioning. Until recently, the owner had been tracking the technicians' hours manually in a log. You have created an Excel worksheet to track the following basic information: service date, technician name, job #, job category, hours, and warranty information. The owner has asked you to analyze the billing data to provide information about the number of hours being spent on the various job categories. He also wants to find out how much of the technicians' work is covered by warranties. You will create a PivotTable that sums the hours by category and technician. Once the table is completed, you will create a column chart representing the billing information.

   a. Start Excel, open the file titled EX L-3.xlsx from the location where you store your Data Files, then save it as **EX L-Service**.

   b. Create a PivotTable on a separate worksheet that sums hours by technician and category. Use **FIGURE L-27** as a guide.

   c. Name the new sheet **PivotTable**, and apply the Pivot Style Medium 14.

   d. Add slicers to filter the PivotTable using the category and technician data. Display only service data for Randal's category Level 1 jobs. Remove the filters, and remove the slicers.

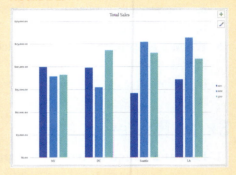

FIGURE L-24

	A	B	C	D	E	F
1						
2	Region	(All)				
3						
4	Sum of Sales					
5		100	200	300	Grand Total	
6	NY	$19,953.00	$17,906.00	$18,254.00	$56,113.00	
7	DC	$19,811.00	$15,472.00	$23,588.00	$58,871.00	
8	Seattle	$14,240.00	$25,424.00	$23,001.00	$62,665.00	
9	LA	$17,181.00	$26,369.00	$21,669.00	$65,219.00	
10	Grand Total	$71,185.00	$85,171.00	$86,512.00	$242,868.00	
11						
12						
13						

FIGURE L-25

FIGURE L-26

	A	B	C	D	E	F
1	Product ID	Region	Store	Sales	Sales Rep	
2	100	West	LA	$11,934	H. Jones	
3	200	West	LA	$16,515	H. Jones	
4	300	West	LA	$18,411	H. Jones	
5	100	East	NY	$12,538	K. Lyons	
6	200	East	NY	$6,052	K. Lyons	
7	300	East	NY	$9,000	K. Lyons	
8	100	West	Seattle	$12,098	M. Hale	
9	200	West	Seattle	$15,550	M. Hale	
10	300	West	Seattle	$17,690	M. Hale	
11	100	East	DC	$11,850	J. Follen	
12	200	East	DC	$14,225	J. Follen	
13	300	East	DC	$18,254	J. Follen	
14	100	West	LA	$5,247	D. Jacobs	
15	200	West	LA	$9,854	D. Jacobs	
16	300	West	LA	$3,258	D. Jacobs	
17	100	East	NY	$7,415	L. Sorelle	
18	200	East	NY	$11,854	L. Sorelle	
19	300	East	NY	$9,254	L. Sorelle	
20	100	West	Seattle	$2,142	T. Leonard	
21	200	West	Seattle	$9,874	T. Leonard	
22	300	West	Seattle	$5,311	T. Leonard	
23	100	East	DC	$7,961	M. Grey	
24	200	East	DC	$1,247	M. Grey	
25	300	East	DC	$5,334	M. Grey	
26						
27			LA Sales for July:	$65,219		
28						
29						
30						

FIGURE L-27

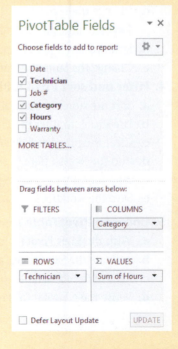

Independent Challenge 1 (continued)

e. Add the Warranty field to the FILTERS area of the PivotTable. Display only the PivotTable data for jobs covered by warranties.

f. Remove the headers of "Column Labels" and "Row Labels" from the PivotTable.

g. Create a clustered column PivotChart that shows the warranty hours. Move the PivotChart to a new sheet named **PivotChart**.

h. Add the title **Warranty Hours** above the chart.

i. Change the PivotChart filter to display hours where the work was not covered by a warranty. Edit the chart title to read **Nonwarranty Hours**.

j. Hide the field buttons on the chart.

k. Add your name to the center section of the PivotTable and PivotChart footers, then save the workbook. Preview the PivotTable and the PivotChart. Close the workbook and exit Excel. Submit the workbook to your instructor.

Independent Challenge 2

You are the owner of an office supply store called Buffalo Office Supplies. You sell products at the store as well as online. You also take orders by phone from your catalog customers. You have been using Excel to maintain a sales summary for the second quarter sales of the different types of products sold by the company. You want to create a PivotTable to analyze and graph the sales in each product category by month and type of order.

a. Start Excel, open the file titled EX L-4.xlsx from the location where you store your Data Files, then save it as **EX L-Office Solutions**.

b. Create a PivotTable on a new worksheet named **PivotTable** that sums the sales amount for each category across the rows and each type of sale down the columns. Add the month field as an inner row label. Use **FIGURE L-28** as a guide.

c. Move the month field to the FILTERS area. Display the sum of sales data for the month of April.

FIGURE L-28

d. Turn off the grand totals for the columns. (*Hint*: Use the Grand Totals button in the Layout group on the PIVOTTABLE TOOLS DESIGN tab and choose On for Rows Only.)

e. Change the summary function in the PivotTable to Average.

f. Format the sales values using the Currency format with two decimal places and the $ symbol. Widen columns C and D to display the sales data.

g. On the Sales worksheet, change the April online paper sales in cell D3 to $20,221. Update the PivotTable to reflect this increase in sales.

h. Sort the average sales of categories from smallest to largest using the grand total of sales.

i. Create a stacked column PivotChart report for the average April sales data for all three types of sales.

j. Change the PivotChart to display the June sales data.

k. Move the PivotChart to a new sheet, and name the chart sheet **PivotChart**.

l. Add the title **Average June Sales** above your chart.

m. On the PivotTable, move the Month field from the FILTERS area to the ROWS area of the PivotTable below the Category field.

n. Add a slicer to filter the PivotTable by month. Use the slicer to display the average sales in April and May.

o. Check the PivotChart to be sure that the filtered data is displayed.

p. Change the chart title to **Average Sales April and May** to describe the charted sales.

q. Add your name to the center section of the PivotTable and PivotChart worksheet footers, save the workbook, then preview the PivotTable and the PivotChart. Close the workbook and exit Excel. Submit the workbook to your instructor.

Excel 2013

Independent Challenge 3

You are the North American sales manager for a drug store supply company with sales offices in the United States and Canada. You use Excel to keep track of the staff in the U.S. and Canadian offices. Management asks you to provide a summary table showing information on your sales staff, including their locations, status, and titles. You will create a PivotTable and PivotChart summarizing this information.

a. Start Excel, open the file titled EX L-5.xlsx from the location where you store your Data Files, then save it as **EX L-Sales Employees**.

b. Create a PivotTable on a new worksheet that shows the number of employees in each city, with the names of the cities listed across the columns, the titles listed down the rows, and the status indented below the titles. (*Hint*: Remember that the default summary function for cells containing text is Count.) Use **FIGURE L-29** as a guide. Rename the new sheet **PivotTable**.

FIGURE L-29

3	Count of Last Name	Column Labels									
4	Row Labels	Baltimore	Charlotte	Chicago	Los Angeles	Montreal	San Francisco	St. Louis	Toronto	Vancouver	Grand Total
5	⊟ Sales Manager	1	2	2	1	1	3	2	3	1	16
6	Full-time		2	2	1	1	2	1	2	1	12
7	Part-time	1					1	1	1		4
8	⊟ Sales Representative	4	7	2	5	4	7	2	3	3	37
9	Full-time	3	5	1	4	3	5	1	2	2	26
10	Part-time	1	2	1	1	1	2	1	1	1	11
11	Grand Total	5	9	4	6	5	10	4	6	4	53

c. Change the structure of the PivotTable to display the data as shown in **FIGURE L-30**.

d. Add a report filter using the Region field. Display only the U.S. employees.

e. Create a clustered column PivotChart from the PivotTable and move the chart to its own sheet named PivotChart. Rearrange the fields to create the PivotChart shown in **FIGURE L-31**.

f. Add the title **U.S. Sales Staff** above the chart.

g. Add the Pivot Style Light 18 style to the PivotTable.

h. Insert a new row in the Employees worksheet above row 7. In the new row, add information reflecting the recent hiring of Kate Conroy, a full-time sales manager at the Baltimore office. Update the PivotTable to display the new employee information.

i. Add the label **Total Chicago Staff** in cell G1 of the Employees sheet. Widen column G to fit the label.

j. Enter a function in cell H1 that retrieves the total number of employees located in Chicago from the PivotTable. Change the page orientation of the Employees sheet to landscape.

k. Use a slicer to filter the PivotTable to display only the data for the cities of Baltimore, Chicago, Los Angeles, and San Francisco.

l. Add another slicer for the Title field to display only the sales representatives.

m. Verify that the number of Chicago employees in cell H1 of the Employees sheet is now 2.

FIGURE L-30

3	Count of Last Name	Column Labels		
4	Row Labels	Full-time	Part-time	Grand Total
5	⊟ Sales Manager	12	4	16
6	Baltimore		1	1
7	Charlotte	2		2
8	Chicago	2		2
9	Los Angeles	1		1
10	Montreal	1		1
11	San Francisco	2	1	3
12	St. Louis	1	1	2
13	Toronto	2	1	3
14	Vancouver	1		1
15	⊟ Sales Representative	26	11	37
16	Baltimore	3	1	4
17	Charlotte	5	2	7
18	Chicago	1	1	2
19	Los Angeles	4	1	5
20	Montreal	3	1	4
21	San Francisco	5	2	7
22	St. Louis	1	1	2
23	Toronto	2	1	3
24	Vancouver	2	1	3
25	Grand Total	38	15	53

FIGURE L-31

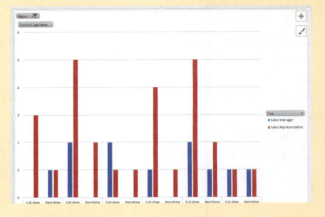

Independent Challenge 3 (continued)

n. Remove the slicers but do not remove the filters.

o. Add your name to the center section of all three worksheet footers, save the workbook, then preview the PivotTable, the first page of the Employees worksheet, and the PivotChart.

p. Close the workbook and exit Excel. Submit the workbook to your instructor.

Independent Challenge 4: Explore

You are the Regional sales manager for a Texas software support company with offices in Austin, Houston, and Dallas. You use Excel to keep track of the revenue generated by sales contracts in these offices. The CEO asks you to provide a summary table showing information on your offices' revenue over the past two years.

a. Start Excel, open the file EX L-6.xlsx, then save it as **EX L-Revenue** in the location where you save your Data Files.

FIGURE L-32

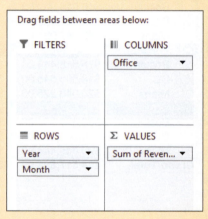

b. Create a PivotTable on a separate worksheet that sums revenue by office, year, and month. Use **FIGURE L-32** as a guide.

c. Name the new sheet **Summary**, and apply the Pivot Style Light 19.

d. Add slicers to filter the PivotTable using the Quarter and Office fields. Display only revenue data for Austin and Dallas for quarters 3 and 4. Remove the filters, but do not remove the slicers.

e. Format the Office slicer using the Slicer Style Light 4 in the Slicer Styles gallery on the SLICER TOOLS OPTIONS tab.

f. Change the Office slicer caption from Office to **Sales Office**. (*Hint*: Use the Slicer Caption text box in the Slicer group of the SLICER TOOLS OPTIONS tab.)

g. Change the Quarter slicer buttons to appear in two columns, with a button height of .3" and a button width of .56". (*Hint*: Use the options in the Buttons group of the SLICER TOOLS OPTIONS tab.)

h. Change the Quarter slicer shape to a height of 1.2" and width of 1.33". (*Hint*: Use the options in the Size group of the SLICER TOOLS OPTIONS tab.) Shorten the Sales Office slicer shape by dragging the lower slicer edge up to just below the bottom button.

i. Add a calculated field named **Average Sale** to the PivotTable to calculate the average sale using the formula =Revenue/Number of Contracts. Change the labels in cells C5, E5, and G5 to **Average** and format all of the Average labels as right justified.

j. Add the Quarter field to the PivotTable as a Report Filter.

k. Copy each quarter's data to a separate sheet. (*Hint*: Select the Quarter field in cell A1, click the Options list arrow in the PivotTable group of the PIVOTTABLE TOOLS ANALYZE tab, then select Show Report Filter Pages.) View the sheet for each quarter.

l. Group all of the worksheets, add your name to the center section of the footer for the worksheets, save the workbook, then preview the worksheets.

m. Close the workbook and exit Excel. Submit the workbook to your instructor.

Visual Workshop

Open the file EX L-7.xlsx from the location where you store your Data Files, then save it as **EX L-Real Estate**. Using the data in the workbook, create the PivotTable shown in FIGURE L-33 on a worksheet named PivotTable, then generate a PivotChart on a new sheet named PivotChart as shown in FIGURE L-34. (*Hint*: The PivotTable has been formatted using the Pivot Style Medium 2. Note that the PivotChart has been filtered.) Add your name to the PivotTable and the PivotChart footers, then preview the PivotTable and the PivotChart. Save the workbook, close the workbook, exit Excel, then submit the workbook to your instructor.

FIGURE L-33

	A	B	C	D	E	F
1						
2						
3	**Sum of Sales**					
4		Jan	Feb	Mar	Grand Total	
5	⊟ Commercial	$17,672,129.00	$18,851,236.00	$31,580,063.00	$68,103,428.00	
6	Boston	$10,018,009.00	$3,115,222.00	$12,025,664.00	$25,158,895.00	
7	DC	$4,711,899.00	$6,605,556.00	$9,504,845.00	$20,822,300.00	
8	Miami	$2,942,221.00	$9,130,458.00	$10,049,554.00	$22,122,233.00	
9	⊟ Land	$120,067,314.00	$165,020,142.00	$96,586,350.00	$381,673,806.00	
10	Boston	$75,518,444.00	$51,027,452.00	$41,025,444.00	$167,571,340.00	
11	DC	$18,505,645.00	$32,503,133.00	$37,515,452.00	$88,524,230.00	
12	Miami	$26,043,225.00	$81,489,557.00	$18,045,454.00	$125,578,236.00	
13	⊟ Residential	$76,578,375.00	$117,522,506.00	$182,574,063.00	$376,674,944.00	
14	Boston	$40,027,554.00	$29,011,550.00	$76,020,776.00	$145,059,880.00	
15	DC	$16,505,377.00	$68,508,511.00	$65,504,845.00	$150,518,733.00	
16	Miami	$20,045,444.00	$20,002,445.00	$41,048,442.00	$81,096,331.00	
17	**Grand Total**	**$214,317,818.00**	**$301,393,884.00**	**$310,740,476.00**	**$826,452,178.00**	
18						
19						
20						
21						
22						

FIGURE L-34

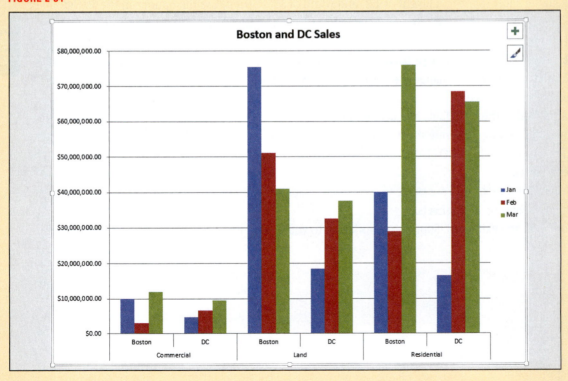

Exchanging Data with Other Programs

CASE ▶ Quest's upper management has asked Kate Morgan, the vice president of sales, to research the possible purchase of Service Adventures, a small company specializing in combining travel with volunteer work for corporate employees. Kate is reviewing the organization's files and developing a presentation on the feasibility of acquiring the company. She asks you to help set up the data exchange between Excel and other programs.

Unit Objectives

After completing this unit, you will be able to:

- Plan a data exchange
- Import a text file
- Import a database table
- Insert a graphic file in a worksheet

- Embed a workbook in a Word document
- Link a workbook to a Word document
- Link an Excel chart to a PowerPoint slide
- Import a table into Access

Files You Will Need

EX M-1.txt	EX M-13.pptx
EX M-2.accdb	EX M-14.xlsx
EX M-3.jpg	EX M-15.xlsx
EX M-4.docx	EX M-16.pptx
EX M-5.xlsx	EX M-17.txt
EX M-6.pptx	EX M-18.docx
EX M-7.xlsx	EX M-19.xlsx
EX M-8.xlsx	EX M-20.docx
EX M-9.txt	EX M-21.xlsx
EX M-10.accdb	EX M-22.xlsx
EX M-11.jpg	EX M-23.accdb
EX M-12.xlsx	

Plan a Data Exchange

Learning Outcomes
- Plan a data exchange between Office programs
- Develop an understanding of data exchange vocabulary

Because the tools available in Microsoft Office programs are designed to be compatible, exchanging data between Excel and other programs is easy. The first step involves planning what you want to accomplish with each data exchange. **CASE** > *Kate asks you to use the following guidelines to plan data exchanges between Excel and other programs in order to complete the business analysis project.*

DETAILS

To plan an exchange of data:

- **Identify the data you want to exchange, its file type, and, if possible, the program used to create it**

  Whether the data you want to exchange is a graphics file, a database file, a worksheet, or consists only of text, it is important to identify the data's **source program** (the program used to create it) and the file type. Once you identify the source program, you can determine options for exchanging the data with Excel. Kate needs to analyze a text file containing the Service Adventures tour sales. Although she does not know the source program, Kate knows that the file contains unformatted text. A file that consists of text but no formatting is sometimes called an **ASCII** or **text** file. Because ASCII is a universally accepted file format, Kate can easily import an ASCII file into Excel. See **TABLE M-1** for a partial list of other file formats that Excel can import.

- **Determine the program with which you want to exchange data**

  Besides knowing which program created the data you want to exchange, you must also identify which program will receive the data, called the **destination program**. This determines the procedure you use to perform the exchange. You might want to insert a graphic object into an Excel worksheet or add a spreadsheet to a Word document. Kate received a database table of Service Adventures' corporate customers created with the Access database program. After determining that Excel can import Access tables and reviewing the import procedure, she imports the database file into Excel so she can analyze it using Excel tools.

- **Determine the goal of your data exchange**

  Windows offers two ways to transfer data within and between programs that allow you to retain some connection with the source program. These data transfer methods use a Windows feature known as **object linking and embedding**, or **OLE**. The data to be exchanged, called an **object**, may consist of text, a worksheet, or any other type of data. You use **embedding** to insert a copy of the original object into the destination document and, if necessary, to then edit this data separately from the source document. This process is illustrated in **FIGURE M-1**. You use **linking** when you want the information you inserted to be updated automatically if the data in the source document changes. This process is illustrated in **FIGURE M-2**. You learn more about embedding and linking later in this unit. Kate has determined that she needs to use both object embedding and object linking for her analysis and presentation project.

- **Set up the data exchange**

  When you exchange data between two programs, it is often best to start both programs before starting the exchange. You might also want to tile the program windows on the screen either horizontally or vertically so that you can see both during the exchange. You will work with Excel, Word, Access, and PowerPoint when exchanging data for this project.

- **Execute the data exchange**

  The steps you use will vary, depending on the type of data you want to exchange. Kate is ready to have you start the data exchanges for the business analysis of Service Adventures.

FIGURE M-1: Embedded object

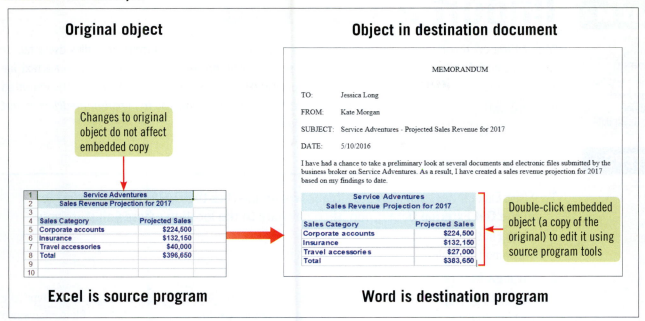

FIGURE M-2: Linked object

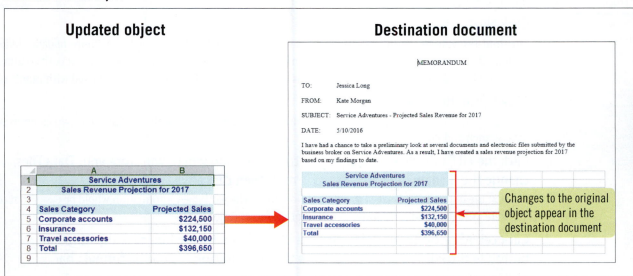

TABLE M-1: File formats Excel can import

file format	file extension(s)	file format	file extension(s)
Access	.mdb, .accdb	All Data Sources	.odc, .udl, .dsn
Text	.txt, .prn, .csv, .dif, .sylk	OpenDocument Spreadsheet	.ods
Query	.iqy, .dqy, .oqy, .rqy	XML	.xml
Web page	.htm, .html, .mht, .mhtml	dBASE	.dbf

Import a Text File

Learning Outcomes
- Import a text file into an Excel workbook
- Format text data

You can import text data into Excel and save the imported data in Excel format. Text files use a tab or space as the **delimiter**, or column separator, to separate columns of data. When you import a text file into Excel, the Text Import Wizard automatically opens and describes how text is separated in the imported file. **CASE** ▶ *Now that Kate has planned the data exchange, she wants you to import a tab-delimited text file containing branch and profit data from Service Adventures.*

STEPS

1. **Start Excel if necessary, create a blank workbook, click the DATA tab, click From Text in the Get External Data group, then navigate to the location where you store your Data Files**

   The Import Text File dialog box shows only text files.

2. **Click EX M-1.txt, then click Import**

   The first Text Import Wizard dialog box opens, as shown in **FIGURE M-3**. Under Original data type, the Delimited option button is selected. In the Preview of file box, line 1 indicates that the file contains two columns of data: Branch and Profit. No changes are necessary in this dialog box.

3. **Click Next**

   The second Text Import Wizard dialog box opens. Under Delimiters, Tab is selected as the delimiter, indicating that tabs separate the columns of incoming data. The Data preview box contains a line showing where the tab delimiters divide the data into columns.

4. **Click Next**

   The third Text Import Wizard dialog box opens with options for formatting the two columns of data. Under Column data format, the General option button is selected. The Data preview area shows that both columns will be formatted with the General format. This is the best formatting option for text mixed with numbers.

5. **Click Finish, then click OK**

   Excel imports the text file into the blank workbook starting in cell A1 of the worksheet as two columns of data: Branch and Profit.

6. **Click the FILE tab, click Save, navigate to the location where you store your Data Files, change the filename to EX M-Branch Profit, then click Save**

   The text file information is saved as an Excel workbook. The worksheet information would be easier to read if it were formatted and if it showed the total profit for all regions.

7. **Click cell A8, type Total Profit, click cell B8, click the HOME tab, click the AutoSum button in the Editing group, then click the Enter button ✔ on the formula bar**

8. **Rename the sheet tab Profit, center the column labels, apply bold formatting to them, format the data in column B using the Currency style with the $ symbol and no decimal places, then click cell A1**

   FIGURE M-4 shows the completed worksheet, which analyzes the text file data you imported into Excel.

9. **Add your name to the center section of the worksheet footer, save the workbook, preview the worksheet, close the workbook, then submit the workbook to your instructor**

FIGURE M-3: First Text Import Wizard dialog box

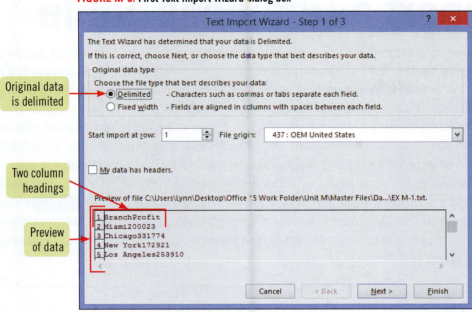

Original data is delimited

Two column headings

Preview of data

FIGURE M-4: Completed worksheet with imported text file

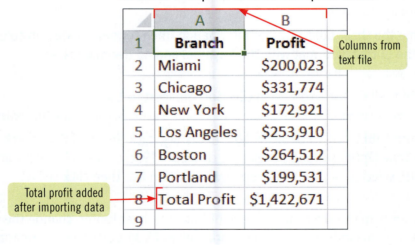

Total profit added after importing data

Columns from text file

Importing files using other methods

Another way to open the Text Import Wizard to import a text file into Excel is to click the FILE tab, click Open, then navigate to the location where you store your Data Files. In the Open dialog box you will see only files that match the file types listed in the Files of type box—usually Microsoft Excel files. To import a text file, you need to change the file type: click All Excel Files, click Text Files (*.prn; *.txt; *.csv), click the text file name, then click Open. You can also drag the icon representing a text file on the Windows desktop into a blank worksheet window. Excel will create a worksheet from the data without using the Wizard.

Import a Database Table

In addition to importing text files, you can also use Excel to import data from database tables. A **database table** is a set of data organized using columns and rows that is created in a database program. A **database program** is an application, such as Microsoft Access, that lets you manage large amounts of data organized in tables. **FIGURE M-5** shows an Access table. To import data from an Access table into Excel, you can copy the table in Access and paste it into an Excel worksheet. This method places a copy of the Access data into Excel; if you change the data in the Access file, the data will not change in the Excel copy. If you want the data in Excel to update when you edit the Access source file, you create a connection, or a **link**, to the database. This lets you work with current data in Excel without recopying the data from Access whenever the Access data changes. **CASE** *Kate received a database table containing Service Adventures' corporate customer information, which was created with Access. She asks you to import this table into an Excel workbook. She would also like you to format, sort, and total the data.*

STEPS

1. **Click the File Tab, click New, then click Blank workbook**
   A new workbook opens, displaying a blank worksheet for you to use to import the Access data.

2. **Click the DATA tab, click the From Access button in the Get External Data group, then navigate to the location where you store your Data Files**

3. **Click EX M-2.accdb, click Open, verify that the Table option button and the Existing worksheet button are selected in the Import Data dialog box, then click OK**
   Excel inserts the Access data into the worksheet as a table with the table style Medium 2 format applied, as shown in **FIGURE M-6**.

4. **Rename the sheet tab Customer Information, then format the data in columns F and G with the Currency format with the $ symbol and no decimal places**
   You are ready to sort the data using the values in column G.

5. **Click the cell G1 list arrow, then click Sort Smallest to Largest**
   The records are reorganized in ascending order according to the amount of the 2017 orders.

6. **Click the TABLE TOOLS DESIGN tab if necessary, click the Total Row check box in the Table Style Options group to select it, click cell F19, click the cell F19 list arrow next to cell F19, select Sum from the drop-down function list, then click cell A1**
   Your completed worksheet should match **FIGURE M-7**.

7. **Add your name to the center section of the worksheet footer, change the worksheet orientation to landscape, save the workbook as EX M-Customer Information, then preview the worksheet**

FIGURE M-5: Access Table

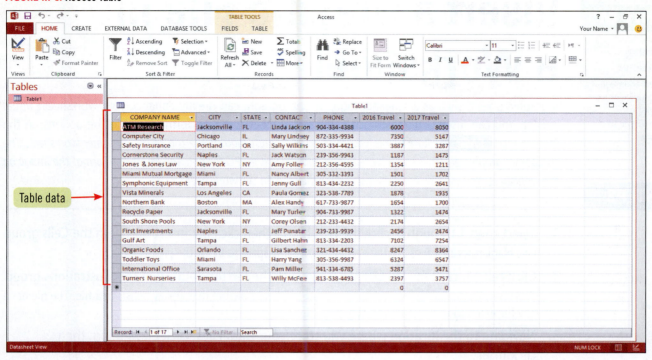

Table data →

FIGURE M-6: Access table imported to Excel

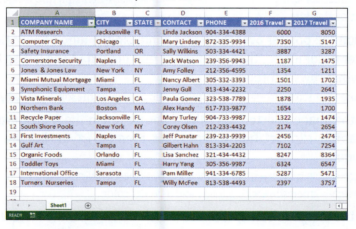

FIGURE M-7: Completed worksheet containing imported data

Data is formatted and sorted in ascending order by 2017 values ←

Totals for 2016 and 2017 orders

Excel 2013

Insert a Graphic File in a Worksheet

A graphic object, such as a drawing, logo, or photograph, can greatly enhance your worksheet's visual impact. You can insert a graphic image into a worksheet and then format it using the options on the Format tab. **CASE** ▶ *Kate wants you to insert the Quest logo at the top of the customer worksheet. The company's graphic designer created the image and saved it in JPG format. You insert and format the image on the worksheet. You start by creating a space for the logo on the worksheet.*

STEPS

1. **Select rows 1 through 5, click the HOME tab, then click the Insert button in the Cells group**
   Five blank rows appear above the header row, leaving space to insert the picture.

2. **Click cell A1, click the INSERT tab, then click the Pictures button in the Illustrations group**
   The Insert Picture dialog box opens. You want to insert a picture that already exists in a file. The file has a .jpg file extension, so it is called a "jay-peg" file.

3. **Navigate to the location where you store your Data Files, click EX M-3.jpg, then click Insert**
   Excel inserts the image and displays the PICTURE TOOLS FORMAT tab. The small circles around the picture's border are sizing handles. Sizing handles appear when a picture is selected; you use them to change the size of a picture.

4. **Position the pointer over the sizing handle in the logo's lower-right corner until the pointer becomes ⬉, then drag the corner up and to the left so that the logo's outline fits within rows 1 through 5**
   Compare your screen to **FIGURE M-8**. You decide to remove the logo's white background.

5. **With the image selected, click the Color button in the Adjust group of the Picture Tools Format tab, click Set Transparent Color, then use ✐ to click the white background on the logo**
   The logo is now transparent, and shows the worksheet gridlines behind it. You decide that the logo will be more visually interesting with a frame and a border color.

6. **With the image selected, click the More button ⬇ in the Picture Styles group, point to several styles and observe the effect on the graphic, click the Reflected Bevel, White style (the third from the right in the last row), click the Picture Border list arrow in the Picture Styles group, then click Blue, Accent 1, Lighter 40% in the Theme Colors group**
   You decide to add a glow to the image.

7. **Click the Picture Effects button in the Picture Styles group, point to Glow, point to More Glow Colors, click Blue, Accent 1, Lighter 80% in the Theme Colors group, resize the logo as necessary to fit it in rows 1 through 5, then drag the logo above the column D data**
   You decide to add an artistic effect to the image.

8. **Click the Artistic Effects button in the Adjust group, click Light Screen (First effect in the third row), then click cell A1**
   Compare your worksheet to **FIGURE M-9**.

9. **Save the workbook, preview the worksheet, close the workbook, exit Excel, then submit the workbook to your instructor**

FIGURE M-8: Resized logo

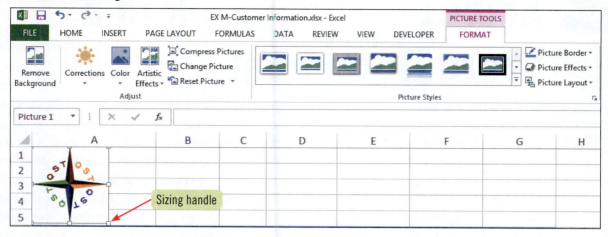

FIGURE M-9: Worksheet with formatted picture

	A	B	C	D	E	F	G	H	I
1									
2									
3						Formatted image			
4									
5									
6	COMPANY NAME	CITY	STATE	CONTACT	PHONE	2016 Travel	2017 Travel		
7	Jones & Jones Law	New York	NY	Amy Folley	212-356-4595	$1,354	$1,211		
8	Recycle Paper	Jacksonville	FL	Mary Turley	904-733-9987	$1,322	$1,474		
9	Cornerstone Security	Naples	FL	Jack Watson	239-356-9943	$1,187	$1,475		

Formatting SmartArt graphics

SmartArt graphics provide another way to visually communicate information on a worksheet. A **SmartArt graphic** is a professionally designed illustration with text and graphics. Each SmartArt type communicates a kind of information or relationship, such as a list, process, or hierarchy. Each type has various layouts you can choose. For example, you can choose from pyramid, process, picture, list, cycle, hierarchy, relationship and matrix layouts, allowing you to illustrate your information in many different ways. To insert a SmartArt graphic into a worksheet, click the INSERT tab, then click the SmartArt button in the Illustrations group. In the Choose a SmartArt Graphic dialog box, choose from eight SmartArt types: List, Process, Cycle, Hierarchy, Relationship, Matrix, Pyramid, and Picture. The dialog box also describes the type of information that is appropriate for each selected layout. After you choose a layout and click OK, a SmartArt object appears on your worksheet. As you enter text in the text entry areas, the font automatically resizes to fit the graphic. The SMARTART TOOLS DESIGN tab lets you choose

color schemes and styles for your SmartArt. You can add effects to SmartArt graphics using choices on the SMARTART TOOLS FORMAT tab. **FIGURE M-10** shows examples of SmartArt graphics. You can create a SmartArt graphic from an existing image by clicking the image, clicking the Picture Layout button in the Picture Styles group of the PICTURE TOOLS FORMAT tab, then selecting the SmartArt type.

FIGURE M-10: Examples of SmartArt graphics

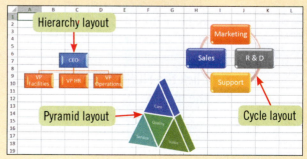

Embed a Workbook in a Word Document

Learning Outcomes
- Embed Excel data in a Word document
- Edit an embedded file icon caption

Microsoft Office programs work together to make it easy to copy an object (such as text, data, or a graphic) in a source program and then insert it into a document in a different program (the destination program). If you insert copied Excel data using a simple Paste command, however, you retain no connection to the source program. That's why it is often more useful to embed objects rather than simply paste them. Embedding allows you to edit an Excel workbook from within the source program using that program's commands and tools. If you send a Word document with an embedded workbook to another person, you do not need to send a separate Excel file with it. All the necessary information is embedded in the Word document. When you embed information, you can either display the data itself or an icon representing the data; users double-click the icon to view the embedded data. An icon is often used rather than the data when the worksheet data is too large to fit well on a Word document. **CASE** ▶ *Kate decides to update Jessica Long, the CEO of Quest, on the project status. She asks you to prepare a Word memo that includes the projected sales workbook embedded as an icon. You begin by starting Word and opening the memo.*

STEPS

1. **Open a File Explorer window, navigate to the location where you store your Data Files, then double-click the file EX M-4.docx to open the file in Word**

   The memo opens in Word.

2. **Click the FILE tab, click Save As, navigate to the location where you store your Data Files, change the file name to EX M-Service Adventures Memo, then click Save**

   You want to embed the workbook below the last line of the document.

3. **Press [Ctrl][End], click the INSERT tab, click the Object button in the Text group, then click the Create from File tab**

   FIGURE M-11 shows the Create from File tab in the Object dialog box. You need to indicate the file you want to embed.

4. **Click Browse, navigate to the location where you store your Data Files, click EX M-5.xlsx, click Insert, then select the Display as icon check box**

   You will change the icon label to a more descriptive name.

5. **Click Change Icon, select the text in the Caption text box, type Projected Sales, click OK twice, then click anywhere in the Word document**

   The memo contains an embedded copy of the sales projection data, displayed as an icon, as shown in **FIGURE M-12**.

6. **Double-click the Projected Sales icon on the Word memo, then maximize the Excel window and the worksheet window if necessary**

   The Excel program starts and displays the embedded worksheet, with its location displayed in the title bar, as shown in **FIGURE M-13**. Any changes you make to the embedded object using Excel tools are not reflected in the source document. Similarly, if you open the source document in the source program, changes you make are not reflected in the embedded copy.

7. **Click the FILE tab, click Close, exit Excel, click the Word FILE tab, then click Save to save the memo**

FIGURE M-11: Object dialog box

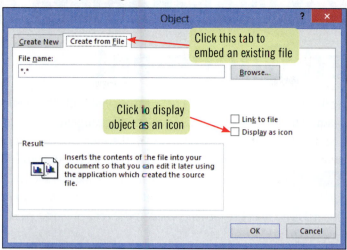

FIGURE M-12: Memo with embedded worksheet displayed as an icon

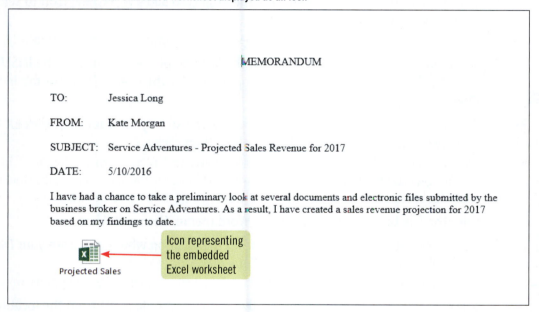

FIGURE M-13: Embedded worksheet open in Excel

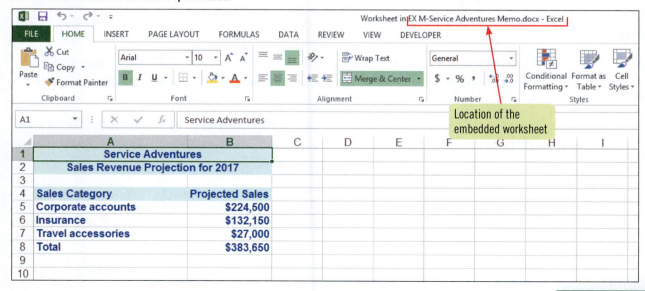

Link a Workbook to a Word Document

Learning Outcomes
• Link data from an Excel worksheet to a Word document
• Update links in a Word document

Linking a workbook to another file retains a connection with the original document as well as the original program. When you link a workbook to another program, the link contains a connection to the source document so that, when you double-click it, the source document opens for editing. In addition, any changes you make to the original workbook (the source document) are reflected in the linked object. **CASE** ▶ *Kate realizes she may need to edit the workbook she embedded in the memo to Jessica. To ensure that these changes will be reflected in the memo, she feels you should use linking instead of embedding. She asks you to delete the embedded worksheet icon and replace it with a linked version of the same workbook.*

STEPS

1. **With the Word memo still open, click the Projected Sales Worksheet icon to select it if necessary, then press [Delete]**

   The workbook is no longer embedded in the memo. The linking process is similar to embedding.

2. **Make sure the insertion point is below the last line of the memo, click the INSERT tab, click the Object button in the Text group, then click the Create from File tab in the Object dialog box**

3. **Click Browse, navigate to the location where you store your Data Files, click EX M-5.xlsx, click Insert, select the Link to file check box, then click OK**

   The memo now displays a linked copy of the sales projection data, as shown in **FIGURE M-14**. In the future, any changes made to the source file, EX M-5, will also be made to the linked copy in the Word memo. You verify this by making a change to the source file and viewing its effect on the memo.

4. **Click the File tab, click Save, close the Word memo, then exit Word**

5. **Start Excel, open the file EX M-5.xlsx from the location where you store your Data Files, click cell B7, type 40000, then press [Enter]**

   You want to verify that the same change was made automatically to the linked copy of the workbook.

6. **Start Word, open the EX M-Service Adventures Memo.docx file from the location where you store your Data Files, then click Yes if asked if you want to update the document's links**

   The memo displays the new value for Travel accessories, and the total has been updated as shown in **FIGURE M-15**.

7. **Click the INSERT tab, click the Header button in the Header & Footer group, click Edit Header, type your name in the Header area, then click the Close Header and Footer button in the Close group**

8. **Save the Word memo, preview it, close the file, exit Word, then submit the file to your instructor**

9. **Close the Excel worksheet without saving it, then exit Excel**

FIGURE M-14: Memo with linked worksheet

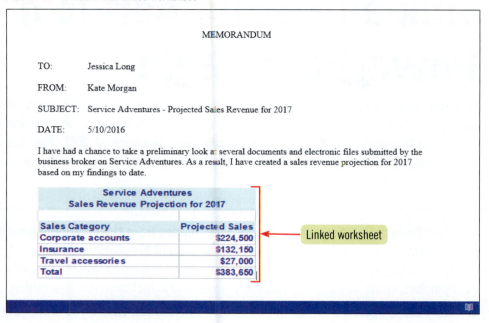

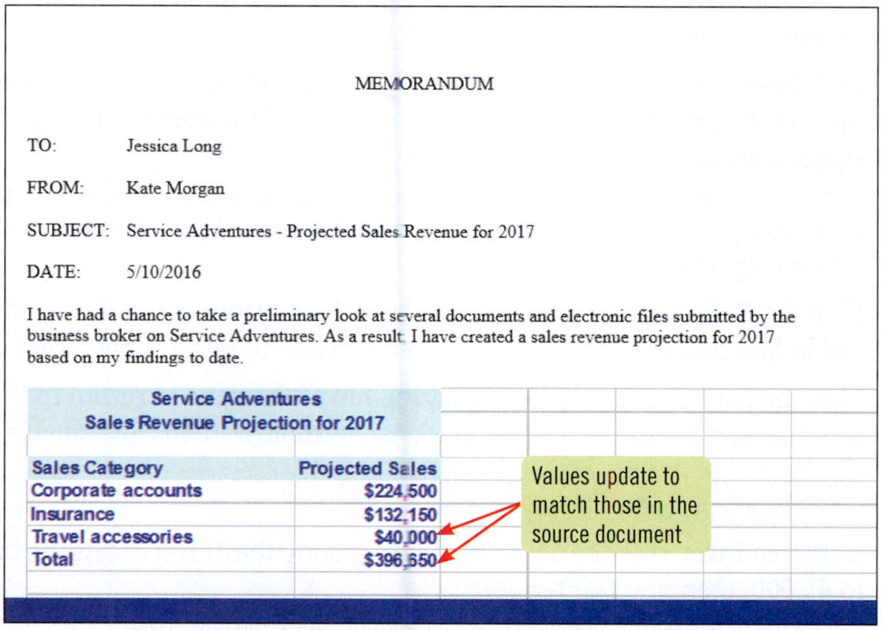

FIGURE M-15: Memo with updated values

Managing links

When you open a document containing linked data, you are asked if you want to update the linked data. You can manage the updating of links by clicking the FILE tab, and clicking Edit Links to Files in the right pane. The Links dialog box opens, allowing you to change a link's update from the default setting of automatic to manual. The Links dialog box also allows you to change the link source, permanently break a link, open the source file, and manually update a link. If you send your linked files to another user, the links will be broken because the linked file path references the local machine where you inserted the links. Because the file path will not be valid on the recipient user's machine, the links will no longer be updated when the user opens the destination document. To correct this, recipients who have both the destination and source documents can use the Links dialog box to change the link's source in the destination document to their own machines. Then the links will be automatically updated when they open the destination document in the future.

Excel 2013

Learning Outcomes
- Link an Excel chart to a PowerPoint slide
- Configure automatic links in a PowerPoint file

Link an Excel Chart to a PowerPoint Slide

Microsoft PowerPoint is a **presentation graphics** program that you can use to create slide show presentations. PowerPoint slides can include a mix of text, data, and graphics. Adding an Excel chart to a slide can help to illustrate data and give your presentation more visual appeal. **CASE** ▶ *Kate asks you to add an Excel chart to one of the PowerPoint slides, illustrating the 2017 sales projection data. She wants you to link the chart in the PowerPoint file.*

STEPS

1. **Start PowerPoint, then open the file EX M-6.pptx from the location where you store your Data Files, then save it as EX M-Management Presentation**

   The presentation appears in Normal view and contains three panes, as shown in **FIGURE M-16**. You need to open the Excel file and copy the chart that you will paste in the PowerPoint presentation.

TROUBLE

If you don't see Copy on the shortcut menu, you may have clicked the Plot area rather than the Chart area. Clicking the white area surrounding the pie will display the Copy command on the menu.

2. **Start Excel, open the file EX M-7.xlsx from the location where you store your Data Files, right-click the Chart Area on the Sales Categories sheet, click Copy on the shortcut menu, then click the PowerPoint program button on the taskbar to display the presentation**

   You need to add an Excel chart to Slide 2, "2017 Sales Projections". To add the chart, you first need to select the slide on which it will appear.

3. **Click Slide 2 in the Thumbnails pane, right-click Slide 2 in the Slide pane, then click the Use Destination Theme & Link Data button (third from the right) in the Paste Options group**

   A pie chart illustrating the 2017 sales projections appears in the slide. The chart matches the colors and fonts in the presentation, which is the destination document. You decide to edit the link so it will update automatically if the data source changes.

QUICK TIP

The default setting for updating links in a PowerPoint file is Manual.

4. **Click the FILE tab, click Edit Links to Files at the bottom of the right pane, in the Links dialog box click the Automatic Update check box to select it, then click Close**

5. **Click the Back to arrow button ◀ at the top of the pane to return to the presentation, click the Save button 🖫 on the Quick Access toolbar, then close the file**

   Kate has learned that the sales projections for the Travel accessories category has increased based on late sales for the current year.

6. **Switch to Excel, click the Sales sheet tab, change the Travel accessories value in cell B7 to 45,000, then press [Enter]**

   You decide to reopen the PowerPoint presentation to check the chart data.

QUICK TIP

To update links in an open PowerPoint file, click the FILE tab, click Edit Links to Files in the right pane, click the link in the Links list, click Update now, then click Close.

7. **Switch to PowerPoint, open the file EX M-Management Presentation.pptx, click Update Links, click Slide 2 in the Thumbnails pane, then point to the Travel accessories pie slice**

   The ScreenTip shows that the chart has updated to display the revised Travel accessories value, $45,000, you entered in the Excel workbook. Slide Show view displays the slide on the full screen the way the audience will see it.

8. **Click the Slide Show button 🖵 on the status bar**

   The finished sales projection slide is complete, as shown in **FIGURE M-17**.

9. **Press [Esc] to return to Normal view; with Slide 2 selected click the Insert tab, click the Header & Footer button in the Text group, select the Footer check box, type your name in the Footer text box, click Apply to All, save and close the presentation, close the Excel file without saving it, exit PowerPoint and Excel, then submit the file to your instructor**

FIGURE M-16: Presentation in Normal view

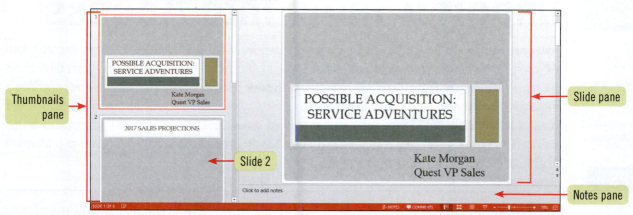

Thumbnails pane

Slide 2

Slide pane

Notes pane

FIGURE M-17: Completed Sales Projections slide in Slide Show view

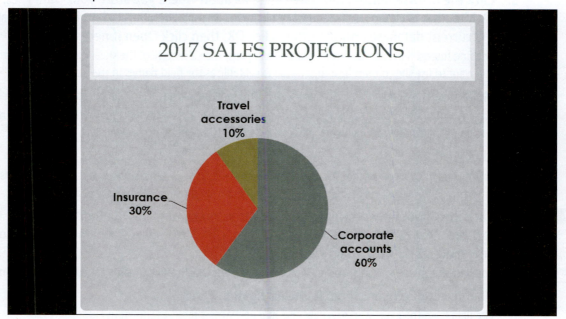

Import a Table into Access

Learning Outcomes
• Import Excel data into an Access database
• Identify a primary key for a database

If you need to analyze Excel data using the more extensive tools of a database, you can import it into Microsoft Access. When you import Excel table data into Access, the data becomes an Access table using the same field names as the Excel table. In the process of importing an Excel table, Access specifies a primary key for the new table. A **primary key** is the field that contains unique information for each record (row) of information. **CASE** *Kate has just received a workbook containing salary information for the managers at Service Adventures, organized in a table. She asks you to convert the Excel table to a Microsoft Access table.*

STEPS

1. **Start Access, click the Blank desktop database button, change the filename in the File Name text box to EX M-SA Management, click the Browse button ☐ next to the filename, navigate to the location where you store your Data Files, click OK, then click Create**

   The database window for the EX M-SA Management database opens. You are ready to import the Excel table data.

2. **Click the EXTERNAL DATA tab, then click the Excel button in the Import & Link group**

   The Get External Data - Excel Spreadsheet dialog box opens, as shown in **FIGURE M-18**. This dialog box allows you to specify how you want the data to be stored in Access.

3. **Click the Browse button, navigate to the location where you store your Data Files, click EX M-8.xlsx, click Open, if necessary click the Import the source data into a new table in the current database option button, click OK, then click Open if necessary**

   The first Import Spreadsheet Wizard dialog box opens, with a sample of the sheet data in the lower section. You want to use the column headings in the Excel table as the field names in the Access database.

4. **Make sure the First Row Contains Column Headings check box is selected, then click Next**

   The Wizard allows you to review and change the field properties by clicking each column in the lower section of the window. You will not make any changes to the field properties.

5. **Click Next**

   The Wizard allows you to choose a primary key for the table. The table's primary key field contains unique information for each record; the ID Number field is unique for each person in the table.

6. **Click the Choose my own primary key option, make sure "ID Number" appears in the text box next to the selected option button, click Next, note the name assigned to the new table, click Finish, then click Close**

   The name of the new Access table ("Compensation") appears in the left pane, called the Navigation pane.

7. **Double-click Compensation: in the Navigation Pane**

   The data from the Excel worksheet appears in a new Access table, as shown in **FIGURE M-19**.

8. **Double-click the border between the Monthly Salary and the Click to Add column headings to widen the Monthly Salary column, then use the last row of the table to enter your name in the First Name and Last Name columns and enter 0 for an ID Number**

9. **Click the Save button ☐ on the Quick Access toolbar, close the file, then exit Access**

FIGURE M-18: Get External Data - Excel Spreadsheet dialog box

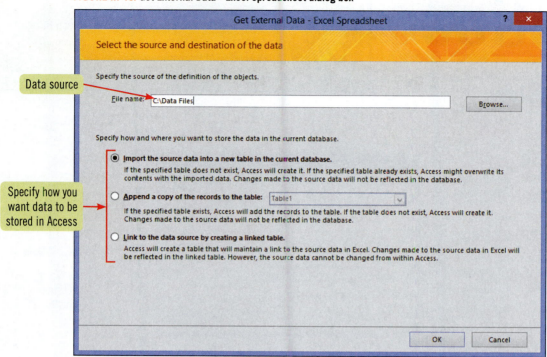

FIGURE M-19: Completed Access table with data imported from Excel

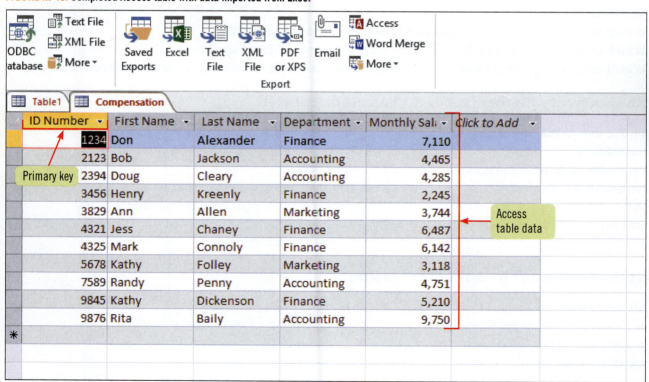

Practice

Concepts Review

FIGURE M-20

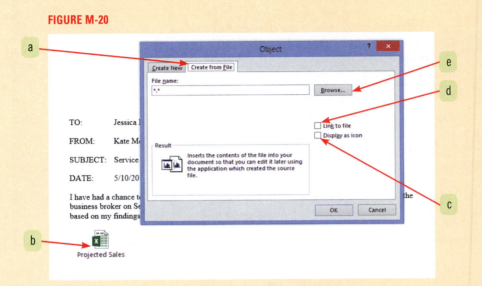

1. Which element do you click to embed information that can be viewed by double-clicking an icon?
2. Which element do you click to insert an existing object into a Word document rather than creating a new file?
3. Which element do you click to find a file to be embedded or linked?
4. Which element do you double-click to display an embedded Excel workbook?
5. Which element do you click to insert an object that maintains a connection to the source document?

Match each term with the statement that best describes it.

6. Source document
7. Embedding
8. Presentation graphics program
9. Destination document
10. OLE
11. Linking

a. File from which the object to be embedded or linked originates
b. Copies an object and retains a connection with the source program and source document
c. Document receiving the object to be embedded or linked
d. Data transfer method used in Windows programs
e. Copies an object and retains a connection with the source program only
f. Used to create slide shows

Select the best answer from the list of choices.

12. An ASCII file:
   a. Contains formatting but no text.
   b. Contains text but no formatting.
   c. Contains a PowerPoint presentation.
   d. Contains an unformatted worksheet.
13. An object consists of:
   a. Text, a worksheet, or any other type of data.
   b. A worksheet only.
   c. Text only.
   d. Database data only.
14. A column separator in a text file is called a(n):
   a. Object.
   b. Link.
   c. Primary key.
   d. Delimiter.

15. To view a workbook that has been embedded as an icon in a Word document, you need to:

a. Double-click the icon.

b. Drag the icon.

c. Click View, then click Worksheet.

d. Click File, then click Open.

16. A field that contains unique information for each record in a database table is called a(n):

a. Primary key.

b. ID Key.

c. First key.

d. Header key.

Skills Review

1. Import a text file.

a. Start Excel, open the tab-delimited text file titled EX M-9.txt from the location where you store your Data Files, then save it as a Microsoft Office Excel workbook with the name **EX M-East Campus Tea**.

b. Format the data in columns B and C using the Currency style with two decimal places.

c. Widen the columns if necessary so that all the data is visible.

d. Center the column labels and apply bold formatting, as shown in **FIGURE M-21**.

e. Add your name to the center section of the worksheet footer, save the workbook, preview the worksheet, close the workbook, then submit the workbook to your instructor.

FIGURE M-21

	A	B	C
1	**Item**	**Cost**	**Price**
2	Pot, small	$9.55	$18.50
3	Pot, large	$11.15	$25.00
4	Pot, decorated	$13.55	$23.70
5	Pot, china	$21.15	$30.90
6	Basket, small	$15.95	$26.80
7	Basket, large	$21.80	$32.90
8	Kettle, small	$16.75	$27.45
9	Kettle, large	$25.30	$33.75
10	Mug, large	$2.95	$4.70
11			

2. Import a database table.

a. Open a blank workbook in Excel, use the From Access button in the Get External Data group on the DATA tab to import the Access Data File EX M-10.accdb from the location where you store your Data Files, then save it as a Microsoft Excel workbook named **EX M-February Budget**.

b. Rename the sheet with the imported data **Budget**.

c. Delete the first data record in row 2.

d. Add a total row to the table to display the sum of the budgeted amounts in cell D25.

e. Apply the Medium 6 Table Style. Format range D2:D25 using the Currency style, the $ symbol, and two decimal places.

f. Save the workbook, and compare your screen to **FIGURE M-22**.

FIGURE M-22

	A	B	C	D
1	Category	Item	Month	Amount
2	Compensation	Bonuses	Feb	$28,147.00
3	Compensation	Commissions	Feb	$22,574.00
4	Compensation	Conferences	Feb	$74,587.00
5	Compensation	Promotions	Feb	$62,354.00
6	Compensation	Payroll Taxes	Feb	$17,887.00
7	Compensation	Salaries	Feb	$42,057.00
8	Compensation	Training	Feb	$58,741.00
9	Facility	Lease	Feb	$47,324.00
10	Facility	Maintenance	Feb	$62,478.00
11	Facility	Other	Feb	$57,148.00
12	Facility	Rent	Feb	$77,634.00
13	Facility	Telephone	Feb	$62,748.00
14	Facility	Utilities	Feb	$57,964.00
15	Supplies	Food	Feb	$61,775.00
16	Supplies	Computer	Feb	$43,217.00
17	Supplies	General Office	Feb	$47,854.00
18	Supplies	Other	Feb	$56,741.00
19	Supplies	Outside Services	Feb	$41,874.00
20	Equipment	Computer	Feb	$49,874.00
21	Equipment	Other	Feb	$43,547.00
22	Equipment	Cash Registers	Feb	$55,987.00
23	Equipment	Software	Feb	$63,147.00
24	Equipment	Telecommunications	Feb	$58,779.00
25	**Total**			$1,194,438.00

Budget ⊕

3. Insert a graphic file in a worksheet.

a. Add four rows above row 1 to create space for an image.

b. In rows 1 through 4, insert the picture file EX M-11.jpg from the location where you store your Data Files.

c. Resize and reposition the picture as necessary to make it fit in rows 1 through 4.

d. Apply the Beveled Matte, White Picture Style, and change the border color to Blue, Accent 5, Lighter 80%. Resize the picture to fit the image and the border in the first four rows. Move the picture to the center of the range A1:D4.

e. Compare your worksheet to **FIGURE M-23**, add your name to the center section of the worksheet footer, preview the workbook, save and close the workbook, then submit the workbook to your instructor.

FIGURE M-23

	A	B	C	D	E	F	G
1							
2							
3							
4							
5	Category	Item	Month	Amount			
6	Compensation	Bonuses	Feb	$28,147.00			
7	Compensation	Commissions	Feb	$22,574.00			
8	Compensation	Conferences	Feb	$74,587.00			
9	Compensation	Promotions	Feb	$62,354.00			
10	Compensation	Payroll Taxes	Feb	$17,887.00			
11	Compensation	Salaries	Feb	$42,057.00			
12	Compensation	Training	Feb	$58,741.00			
13	Facility	Lease	Feb	$47,324.00			
14	Facility	Maintenance	Feb	$62,478.00			
15	Facility	Other	Feb	$57,148.00			
16	Facility	Rent	Feb	$77,634.00			
17	Facility	Telephone	Feb	$62,748.00			
18	Facility	Utilities	Feb	$57,964.00			
19	Supplies	Food	Feb	$61,775.00			

© Burazin/Getty Images

Skills Review (continued)

4. Embed a workbook in a Word document.

   a. Start Word, create a memo with a header addressed to your instructor, enter your name in the From line, enter **February Salaries** as the subject, and enter the current date in the Date line.

   b. In the memo body, enter **The February salaries are provided in the worksheet below**:

   c. In the memo body, use the Object dialog box to embed the workbook EX M-12.xlsx from the location where you store your Data Files, displaying it as an icon with the caption **Salary Details**.

FIGURE M-24

   d. Save the document as **EX M-February Salaries** in the location where you store your Data Files, then double-click the icon to verify that the workbook opens. (*Hint*: If the workbook does not appear after you double-click it, click the Excel icon on the taskbar.)

   e. Close the workbook and return to Word.

   f. Compare your memo to **FIGURE M-24**.

5. Link a workbook to a Word document.

   a. Delete the icon in the memo body.

   b. In the memo body, link the workbook EX M-12.xlsx, displaying the data, not an icon.

   c. Save the document, then note that Mary Glenn's salary is $7,100. Close the document.

   d. Open the EX M-12.xlsx workbook in Excel, and change Mary Glenn's salary to **$7500**.

FIGURE M-25

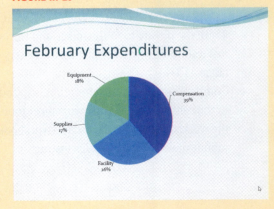

   e. Open the **EX M-February Salaries** document in Word, update the links, and verify that Mary Glenn's salary has changed to $7,500 and that the new total salaries amount is $48,057, as shown in **FIGURE M-25**. (*Hint*: If the dialog box does not open, giving you the opportunity to update the link, then right-click the worksheet object and click Update Link.)

   f. Save the **EX M-February Salaries** document, preview the memo, close the document, exit Word, then submit the document to your instructor.

   g. Close the EX M-12 workbook without saving changes, then exit Excel.

6. Link an Excel chart to a PowerPoint slide.

   a. Start PowerPoint.

   b. Open the PowerPoint file EX M-13.pptx from the location where you store your Data Files, then save it as **EX M-Budget Meeting**.

   c. Display Slide 2, February Expenditures.

FIGURE M-26

   d. Link the chart, using the theme of the destination file, from the Excel file EX M-14.xlsx from the location where you store your Data Files to Slide 2. Edit the link to be updated automatically. Save and close the Ex M-Budget Meeting file.

   e. Change the Equipment amount on Sheet1 of the file EX M-14 to $207,000, open the EX M-Budget Meeting file, updating the links, and verify the Equipment percentage changed from 17% to 18% on Slide 2.

   f. View the slide in Slide Show view.

   g. Press [Esc] to return to Normal view. Resize and reposition the chart to fit on the slide if necessary. Compare your slide to **FIGURE M-26**.

Skills Review (continued)

h. Add a footer to all of the slides with your name.

i. Save the presentation, exit PowerPoint, close EX M-14 without saving it, then submit the presentation to your instructor.

7. Import a table into Access.

a. Start Access.

b. Create a blank desktop database named **EX M-Budget** in the location where you store your Data Files.

FIGURE M-27

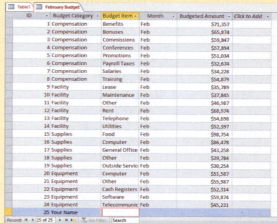

c. Use the EXTERNAL DATA tab to import the Excel table in the file EX M-15.xlsx from the location where you store your Data Files. Store the data in a new table, use the first row as column headings, let Access add the primary key, and use the default table name February Budget.

d. Open the February Budget table in Access, and widen the columns as necessary to fully display the field names and field information.

e. Enter your name in the Budget Category column of row 25 in the table, save the database file, compare your screen to **FIGURE M-27**, exit Access, then submit the database file to your instructor.

Independent Challenge 1

You are a real estate agent for the Naples office of West Coast Realty. You have been asked to give a presentation to the regional manager about your sales in the past month. To illustrate your sales data, you will add an Excel chart to one of your slides, showing the different types of property sales and the sales amounts for each type.

a. Start Excel, create a new workbook, then save it as **EX M-June Sales** in the location where you store your Data Files.

b. Enter the property types and the corresponding sales amounts shown below into the EX M-June Sales workbook. Name the sheet with the sales data **Sales**.

Property Type	Sales
Condominium	$2,300,500
Single-family	$8,100,200
Land	$1,210,000

c. Create a 3-D pie chart from the sales data. Format it using Chart Style 9.

d. Copy the chart to the Clipboard.

e. Start PowerPoint, open the Data File EX M-16.pptx from the location where you store your Data Files, then save it as **EX M-Sales Presentation**.

FIGURE M-28

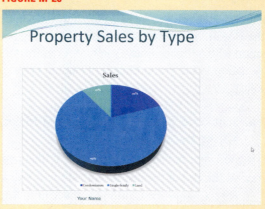

f. Link the Excel chart to Slide 2 using the destination theme. Use the sizing handles to change the size if necessary, and drag the edge of the chart to position it in the center of the slide if necessary.

g. View the slide in Slide Show view, then press [Esc] to end the show.

h. Add a footer to the slides with your name, then save the presentation. Slide 2 should look like **FIGURE M-28**.

i. Change the status of links in the PowerPoint file to update automatically.

j. Close the presentation, exit PowerPoint, then submit the PowerPoint file to your instructor.

k. Save the workbook, then close the workbook, and exit Excel.

Independent Challenge 2

You are opening a new fitness center, Total Sports, in Oakland, California. The owner of a fitness center in the area is retiring and has agreed to sell you a text file containing his list of supplier information. You need to import this text file into Excel so that you can manipulate the data. Later, you will convert the Excel file to an Access table so that you can give it to your business partner who is building a supplier database.

a. Start Excel, import the file EX M-17.txt from the location where you store your Data Files, then save it as an Excel file named **EX M-Fitness Suppliers**. (*Hint*: This is a tab-delimited text file.)

b. Adjust the column widths as necessary. Rename the worksheet **Suppliers**.

c. Sort the worksheet data in ascending order by Supplier.

d. Add your name to the center section of the worksheet footer, save and close the workbook, then exit Excel.

e. Start Access, create a new blank desktop database in the location where you store your Data Files. Name the new database **EX M-Suppliers**.

f. Use the EXTERNAL DATA tab to import the Excel file EX M-Fitness Suppliers from the location where you store your Data Files. Store the data in a new table, use the column labels as the field names, let Access add the primary key, and accept the default table name.

g. Open the Suppliers table and AutoFit the columns.

h. Enter your name in the Supplier column in row 13, then compare your database file to **FIGURE M-29**.

i. Save and then close the table, and exit Access.

j. Submit the database file to your instructor.

FIGURE M-29

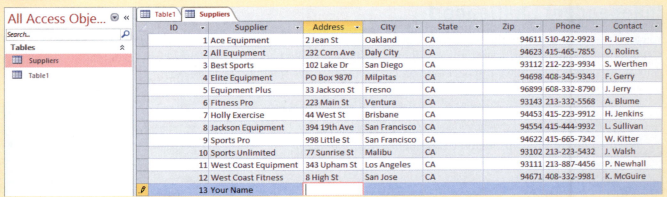

Independent Challenge 3

You are the newly hired manager at NE Financial, a mutual funds firm specializing in consumer products. An employee, Kathy Hogan, has completed a two-year training period as an assistant and you would like to promote her to an associate position with a higher salary. You have examined the salaries of the other associates in the company and will present this information to the vice president of Human Resources, requesting permission to grant Kathy a promotion and an increase in salary.

a. Start Word, open the Word file EX M-18.docx from the location where you store your Data Files, then save it as **EX M-Promotion**.

b. Add your name to the From line of the memo, and change the date to the current date.

c. At the end of the memo, embed the workbook EX M-19.xlsx as an icon from the location where you store your Data Files. Change the caption for the icon to **Salaries**. Double-click the icon to verify that the workbook opens.

d. Close the workbook, return to Word, delete the Salaries icon, and link the workbook EX M-19 to the memo, displaying the data, not an icon.

e. Save the EX M-Promotion memo, and close the file.

f. Open the EX M-19.xlsx workbook in Excel, and change Kathy Hogan's salary to $51,000.

Independent Challenge 3 (continued)

g. Open the EX M-Promotion memo, update the links, and make sure Kathy Hogan's salary is updated.

h. Save and close the memo. Exit Word and submit the memo to your instructor.

i. Close EX M-19 without saving the changes to Karen Holden's information, then exit Excel.

Independent Challenge 4: Explore

You work as a technology manager at a local town office. Each Friday afternoon you are required to submit your hours to your supervisor in a Word document. You prefer to use Excel to track your daily hours so you will link your worksheet to a Word document for your supervisor.

a. Open the file EX M-20.docx from the location where you store your Data Files, then save it as **EX M-Hours**.

b. Change "Your Name" in the FROM line with your own name.

c. Open the file EX M-21.xlsx from the location where you store your Data Files. Copy the range A1:B8 to the Clipboard.

d. Return to the EX M-Hours document, and use the Paste Special in the Paste Options to paste the copied range as a linked worksheet object with the destination style. (*Hint:* Using **FIGURE M-30** as a guide, right-click below the line "My hours for this week are shown below.", then click the Link & Use Destination Styles option in the Paste Options group. It is the 4th option from the left.) Save and close the memo.

FIGURE M-30

e. In the EX M-21 workbook, change Sunday's hours to 5.

f. Return to Word, open the EX M-Hours memo, update links, then verify that the new hours information appears. Save and then close the memo and exit Word. Close the EX M-21 workbook without saving the file and exit Excel.

g. Using Access, create a new blank desktop database named **EX M-Week** in the location where you store your Data Files. Link the Excel data in the EX M-22.xlsx file to the EX M-Week database file using **FIGURE M-31** as a guide. View the data in the linked Hours table by double-clicking the object's name.

h. Close the database file, open the EX M-22.xlsx file, and change the hours for Sunday to 10. Save and close the Excel file.

i. Open the EX M-Week database, verify that the hours figure for Sunday was updated in the linked Hours table, then close the database and exit Access.

j. Submit the EX M-Hours Word document and the EX M-Week database file to your instructor.

FIGURE M-31

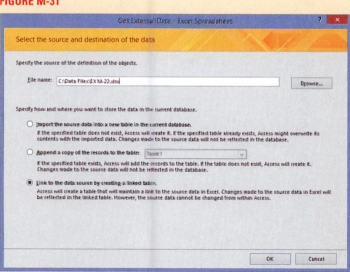

Excel 2013

Visual Workshop

Create the worksheet shown in **FIGURE M-32** by opening a blank workbook, importing the Access data in file EX M-23.accdb, sorting the data in Excel, and formatting the price data. The image is from the Microsoft ClipArt. (*Hint*: Click the Online Pictures button in the Illustrations group of the INSERT tab and search for Dog. If you don't see the image shown, select another. Notice the image's transparent background.) Add your name to the center section of the Prices worksheet. Save the workbook as **EX M-Prices**, close the workbook, then exit Excel. Submit the file to your instructor.

FIGURE M-32

	A	B	C
1			
2			
3			
4			
5			
6	Item Code	Product	Price
7	B755	Cat Post	$18.99
8	B132	Cat Collar	$22.36
9	A135	Dog Collar	$31.19
10	A884	Dog Toy Set	$37.54
11	A252	Dog Brush Set	$39.94
12	B211	Cat Play Set	$52.99
13	A410	Dog Crate Small	$112.57
14	A408	Dog Crate Medium	$115.22
15	B111	Cat Bed	$116.99
16	A327	Dog Bed Small	$130.57
17	A407	Dog Crate Large	$141.99
18	A321	Dog Bed Large	$155.99
19			

Sharing Excel Files and Incorporating Web Information

CASE ▶ Kate Morgan, the vice president of sales for Quest, wants to share information with corporate office employees and branch managers using the company's intranet and the Web. Kate wants the Quest sales department to use shared workbooks to collaborate on sales worksheet data.

Unit Objectives

After completing this unit, you will be able to:

- Share Excel files
- Set up a shared workbook for multiple users
- Track revisions in a shared workbook
- Apply and modify passwords

- Work with XML schemas
- Import and export XML data
- Share Web links
- Import and export HTML data

Files You Will Need

EX N-1.xlsx	EX N-9.xml
EX N-2.xlsx	EX N-10.htm
EX N-3.xsd	EX N-11.xlsx
EX N-4.xml	EX N-12.htm
EX N-5.xml	EX N-13.xsd
EX N-6.htm	EX N-14.xml
EX N-7.xlsx	EX N-15.htm
EX N-8.xsd	

Share Excel Files

Microsoft Excel provides many different ways to share spreadsheets with people in your office, in your organization, or anywhere on the Web. When you share workbooks, you have to consider how you will protect information that you don't want everyone to see and how you can control revisions others will make to your files. Also, some information you want to use might not be in Excel format. For example, there is a great deal of information published on the Web in HTML format, so Excel allows you to import HTML to your worksheets. You can also export your worksheet data in HTML format. However, many companies find the XML format to be more flexible than HTML for storing and exchanging data, so they are increasingly using XML to store and exchange data both internally and externally. Excel allows you to easily import and export XML data. You can also share data using links. **FIGURE N-1** shows methods of importing to and exporting from workbooks. **CASE** ▶ *Kate needs to decide the best way to share her Excel workbooks with corporate employees and branch managers.*

DETAILS

To share worksheet information, consider the following issues:

- #### Allowing others to use a workbook
  While many of your workbooks are for your own use, you will want to share some of them with other users. When users **share** your workbooks, they can simultaneously open them from a network server, modify them electronically, and return their revisions to you for incorporation with others' changes. You can view each user's name and the date each change was made. To share a workbook, you need to turn on the sharing feature for that workbook. Kate wants to obtain feedback on Quest sales data from the branch managers, so she sets up her workbook so others can use it.

- #### Controlling access to workbooks on a server
  When you place a workbook on a network server, you will probably want to control who can open and change it. You can do this using Excel passwords. Kate assigns a password to her workbook, then posts the workbook on the Quest server. She gives the corporate staff and branch managers the password, so only they can open the workbook and revise it.

- #### HTML data
  You can paste data from a Web page into a worksheet and then manipulate and format it using Excel. You can also save Excel workbook information in HTML format so you can publish it on an intranet or on the Web. Kate decides to publish the worksheet with the North American sales information in HTML format on the company intranet, as shown in **FIGURE N-2**.

- #### Working with XML data
  Importing and storing data in XML format allows you to use it in different situations. For example, a company might store all of its sales data in an XML file and make different parts of the file available to various departments such as marketing and accounting. These departments can extract information that is relevant to their purposes from the file. A subset of the same XML file might be sent to vendors or other business associates who only require certain types of sales data stored in the XML file. Kate decides to import XML files that contain sales information from the Miami and New York branches to get a sales summary for Quest's eastern region, as shown in **FIGURE N-3**.

- #### Sharing workbooks in the Cloud
  After you save a workbook on your SkyDrive, you can use Excel sharing tools to email links to your workbook, invite people to access the workbook using the Excel Web App, and even post a workbook link on a social networking site. Kate decides to share the branch sales results with the managers by saving the workbook in the cloud and sending the managers a link to access the information.

Sharing Excel Files and Incorporating Web Information

FIGURE N-1: Importing and exporting data

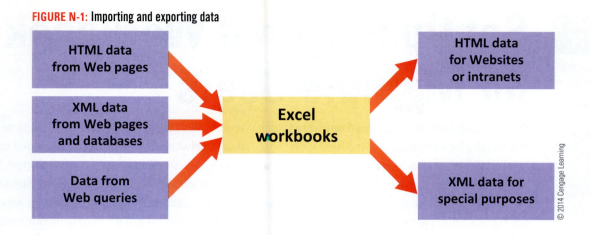

© 2014 Cengage Learning

FIGURE N-2: North America sales information displayed in a Web browser

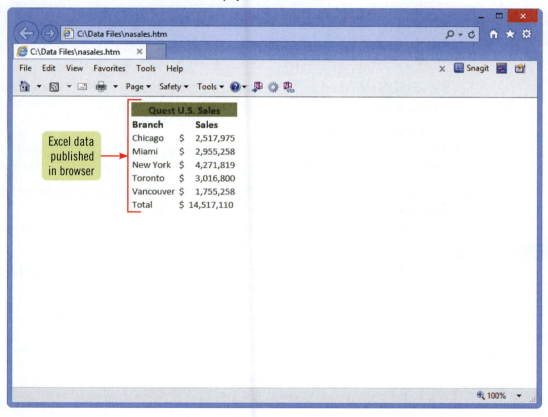

FIGURE N-3: Data imported from XML file

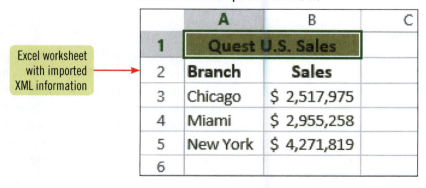

Set Up a Shared Workbook for Multiple Users

You can make an Excel file a **shared workbook** so that several users can open and modify it at the same time. This is useful for workbooks that you want others to review on a network server, where the workbook is equally accessible to all network users. When you share a workbook, you can have Excel keep a list of all changes to the workbook, which you can view and print at any time. Note that not all features are available in shared workbooks. **CASE** *Kate wants to get feedback from selected corporate staff and branch managers before presenting the information at the next corporate staff meeting. She asks you to help her put a shared workbook containing customer and sales data on the company's network. You begin by making her Excel file a shared workbook.*

STEPS

1. **Start Excel, open the file EX N-1.xlsx from the location where you store your Data Files, then save it as EX N-Sales Information**

   The workbook with the sales information opens, displaying two sheet tabs. The first contains tour sales data for the Quest U.S. branches; the second is a breakdown of the branch sales by sales associate.

2. **Click the REVIEW tab, then click the Share Workbook button in the Changes group**

   The Share Workbook dialog box opens, as shown in **FIGURE N-4**.

3. **Click the Editing tab, if necessary**

   The dialog box lists the names of people who are currently using the workbook. You are the only user, so your name, or the name of the person entered as the computer user, appears, along with the current date and time.

4. **Click to select the check box next to Allow changes by more than one user at the same time. This also allows workbook merging., then click OK**

   A dialog box appears, asking if you want to save the workbook. This will resave it as a shared workbook.

5. **Click OK**

   Excel saves the file as a shared workbook. The title bar now reads EX N-Sales Information.xlsx [Shared], as shown in **FIGURE N-5**. This version replaces the unshared version.

Adding Office Apps to a worksheet

To help manage information on your worksheets, you can add an Office App to Excel. The app will be available to use for all of your worksheets. For example, there are maps, dictionaries, and calendars that help personalize your worksheets. To insert an app into Excel, click the INSERT tab, click the Apps for Office list arrow in the Apps group, click See All, click FEATURED APPS, then select the app that you want to insert. Clicking More apps opens an Office store Web page with additional app information. If your app isn't open, click the INSERT tab, click the Apps for Office list arrow in the Apps group, click See All, click MY APPS, select the app that you want to insert, then click Insert. If you have used an app recently, open it by clicking the Apps for Office list arrow and clicking the app name in the Recently Used Apps list. Office Apps are not available in shared workbooks.

FIGURE N-4: Share Workbook dialog box

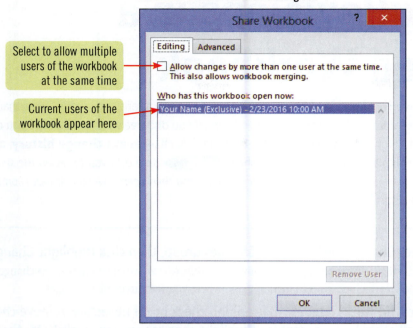

Select to allow multiple users of the workbook at the same time

Current users of the workbook appear here

FIGURE N-5: Shared workbook

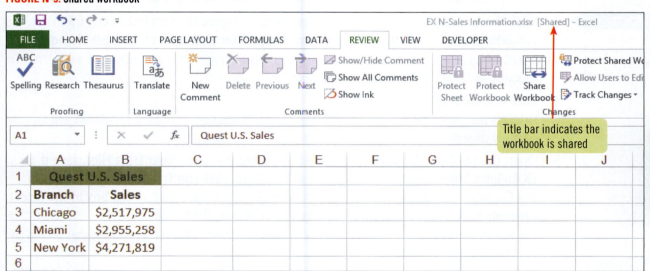

Title bar indicates the workbook is shared

Merging workbooks

Instead of putting the shared workbook on a server to be shared simultaneously, you might want to distribute copies to your reviewers via e-mail. Once everyone has entered their changes and returned their workbook copies to you, you can merge the changed copies into one master workbook that contains everyone's changes. Each copy you distribute must be designated as shared, and the Change History feature on the Advanced tab of the Share Workbook dialog box must be activated. Occasionally a conflict occurs when two users are trying to edit the same cells in a shared workbook. In this case, the second person to save the file will see a Resolve Conflicts dialog box and need to choose Accept

Mine or Accept Other. To merge workbooks, you need to add the Compare and Merge Workbooks command to the Quick Access toolbar by clicking the FILE tab, clicking Options, and clicking Quick Access toolbar. Click All Commands in the Choose commands from list, click Compare and Merge Workbooks, click Add, then click OK. Once you get the changed copies back, open the master copy of the workbook, then click the Compare and Merge Workbooks button on the Quick Access toolbar. The Select Files to Merge Into Current Workbook dialog box opens. Select the workbooks you want to merge (you can use the [Ctrl] key to select more than one workbook), then click OK.

Learning
Outcomes
• Review changes to
  a shared workbook
• Create a change
  history worksheet

Track Revisions in a Shared Workbook

When you share workbooks, it is often helpful to **track** modifications, or identify who made which changes. You can accept the changes you agree with, and if you disagree with any changes you can reject them. In addition to highlighting changes, Excel keeps track of changes in a **change history**, a list of all changes that you can place on a separate worksheet. **CASE** *Kate asks you to set up the shared Sales Information workbook so that Excel tracks all future changes. You then open a workbook that is on the server and review its changes and the change history.*

STEPS

1. **Click the Track Changes button in the Changes group, then click Highlight Changes**

   The Highlight Changes dialog box opens, as shown in **FIGURE N-6**, allowing you to turn on change tracking. You can also specify which changes to highlight and where you want to display changes.

2. **Click to select the Track changes while editing check box if necessary, remove check marks from all other boxes except for Highlight changes on screen, click OK, then click OK in the dialog box that informs you that you have yet to make changes**

   Leaving the When, Who, and Where check boxes blank allows you to track all changes.

   QUICK TIP
   Cells changed by other users appear in different colors.

3. **Click the Sales by Rep sheet tab, change the sales figure for Sanchez in cell C3 to 250,000, press [Enter], then move the mouse pointer over the cell you just changed**

   A border with a small triangle in the upper-left corner appears around the cell you changed, and a ScreenTip appears with the date, the time, and details about the change, as shown in **FIGURE N-7**.

4. **Save and close the workbook**

   Jose Silva has made changes to a version of this workbook. You want to open this workbook and view the details of these changes and accept the ones that appear to be correct.

5. **Open the file EX N-2.xlsx from the location where you store your Data Files, save it as EX N-Sales Information Edits, click the REVIEW tab, click the Track Changes button in the Changes group, click Accept/Reject Changes, click the When check box in the Select Changes to Accept or Reject dialog box to deselect it, then click OK**

   You will accept the first four changes that Jose made to the workbook and reject his last change. You also want to see a list of all changes.

6. **Click Accept four times to approve the first four changes, click Reject to undo Jose's fifth change, click the Track Changes button in the Changes group, click Highlight Changes, click the When check box in the Highlight Changes dialog box to deselect it, click to select the List changes on a new sheet check box, then click OK**

   A new sheet named History opens, as shown in **FIGURE N-8**, with Jose's changes in a filtered list. Because saving the file closes the History sheet, you need to copy the information to a new worksheet.

7. **Copy the range A1:I6 on the History sheet, click the New sheet button ⊕ next to the History sheet tab, on the new sheet click the HOME tab, click the Paste button in the Clipboard group, widen columns E, F, H, and I to display the column information, then rename the new sheet tab Saved History**

   TROUBLE
   You can enter a footer in Page Layout view if the Header & Footer button is not available. Not all commands are available in shared workbooks.

8. **Add a footer with your name to the Saved History sheet, save and close the workbook, then submit the workbook to your instructor**

FIGURE N-6: Highlight Changes dialog box

Select to show changes to the worksheet →

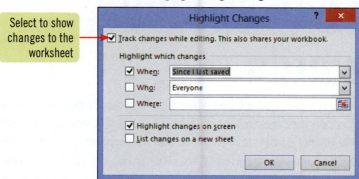

FIGURE N-7: Tracked change

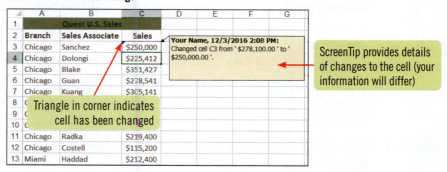

Triangle in corner indicates cell has been changed

ScreenTip provides details of changes to the cell (your information will differ)

FIGURE N-8: History sheet tab with change history

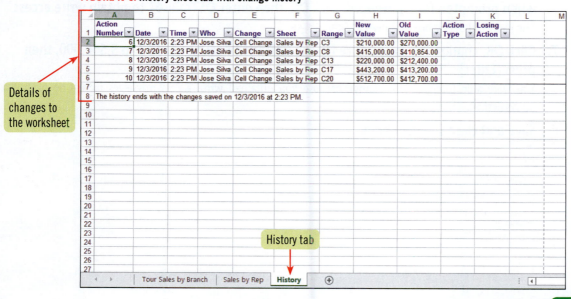

Details of changes to the worksheet

History tab

Excel 2013

Apply and Modify Passwords

Learning Outcomes
- Create a password to open a workbook
- Create a password to modify a workbook

When you place a shared workbook on a server, you may want to use a password so that only authorized people will be able to open it or make changes to it. However, it's important to remember that *if you lose your password, you will not be able to open or change the workbook*. Passwords are case sensitive, so you must type them exactly as you want users to type them, with the same spacing and using the same case. For security, it is a good idea to include uppercase and lowercase letters and numbers in a password. **CASE** ▸ *Kate wants you to put the workbook with sales information on one of the company's servers. You decide to save a copy of the workbook with two passwords: one that users will need to open it, and another that they will use to make changes to it.*

STEPS

QUICK TIP

You can also use a password to encrypt the contents of a workbook: click the FILE tab, click Protect Workbook in the middle pane, click Encrypt with Password, then enter a password.

1. **Open the file EX N-1.xlsx from the location where you store your Data Files, click the FILE tab, click Save As, navigate to the location where you store your Data Files, click the Tools list arrow in the bottom of the Save As dialog box, then click General Options**

   The General Options dialog box opens, with two password boxes: one to open the workbook, and one to allow changes to the workbook, as shown in **FIGURE N-9**. You can also protect data using a password to encrypt it. **Encrypted data** is encoded in a form that only authorized people with a password can decode.

2. **In the Password to open text box, type QSTmanager01**

   Be sure to type the letters in the correct cases. This is the password that users must type to open the workbook. When you enter passwords, the characters you type are masked with bullets (• • •) for security purposes.

QUICK TIP

You can press [Enter] rather than clicking OK after entering a password. This allows you to keep your hands on the keyboard.

3. **Press [Tab], in the Password to modify text box, type QSTsales01, then click OK**

   This is the password that users must type to make changes to the workbook, also referred to as having **write access**. A dialog box asks you to verify the first password by reentering it.

4. **Enter QSTmanager01 in the first Confirm Password dialog box, click OK, enter QSTsales01 in the second Confirm Password dialog box, then click OK**

5. **Change the filename to EX N-Sales Information PW, if necessary navigate to the location where you store your Data Files, click Save, then close the workbook**

QUICK TIP

To delete a password, reopen the General Options dialog box, highlight the symbols for the existing password, press [Delete], click OK, change the filename, then click Save.

6. **Reopen the workbook EX N-Sales Information PW, enter the password QSTmanager01 when prompted for a password, click OK, then enter QSTsales01 to obtain write access**

   The Password dialog box is shown in **FIGURE N-10**.

7. **Click OK, change the sales figure for the Chicago branch in cell B3 to 3,500,000, then press [Enter]**

   You were able to make this change because you obtained write access privileges using the password "QSTsales01".

8. **Save and close the workbook**

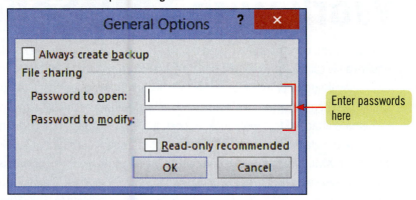

Enter passwords here

Password is masked with bullets for security

Excel 2013

Creating strong passwords for Excel workbooks

Strong passwords will help to protect your workbooks from security threats. A **strong password** has at least 14 characters that are not commonly used. Although your password needs to be easy to remember, it should be difficult for other people to guess. Avoid using your birthday, your pet's name, or other personal information in your password. Also avoid dictionary words and repeated characters. Instead, mix the types of characters using uppercase and lowercase letters, numbers, and special characters such as @ and %. Microsoft offers an online password checker to test your passwords for security. See **TABLE N-1** for rules and examples for creating strong passwords.

TABLE N-1: Rules for creating strong passwords

rule	example
Include numbers	5qRyz8O6w
Add symbols	IQx!u%z7q9
Increase complexity	4!%5Zq^c6#
Use long passwords	Z7#l%2!q9!6@i9&Wb

© 2014 Cengage Learning

Work with XML Schemas

Using Excel you can import and export XML data and analyze it using Excel tools. To import XML data, Excel requires a file called a schema that describes the structure of the XML file. A **schema** contains the rules for the XML file by listing all of the fields in the XML document and their characteristics, such as the type of data they contain. A schema is used to **validate** XML data, making sure the data follows the rules given in the file. Once a schema is attached to a workbook, a schema is called a **map**. When you map an element to a worksheet, you place the element name on the worksheet in a specific location. Mapping XML elements allows you to choose the XML data from a file with which you want to work in the worksheet. **CASE** ▶ *Kate has been given XML files containing sales information from the U.S. branches. She asks you to prepare a workbook to import the sales representatives' XML data. You begin by adding a schema to a worksheet that describes the XML data.*

STEPS

1. **Create a new workbook, save it as EX N-Sales Reps in the location where you store your Data Files, click the DEVELOPER tab, then click the Source button in the XML group**

   The XML Source pane opens. This is where you specify a schema, or map, to import. A schema has the extension .xsd. Kate has provided you with a schema she received from the IT Department describing the XML file structure.

2. **Click XML Maps at the bottom of the task pane**

   The XML Maps dialog box opens, listing the XML maps or schemas in the workbook. There are no schemas in the Sales Reps workbook at this time, as shown in **FIGURE N-11**.

3. **Click Add in the XML Maps dialog box, navigate to the location where you store your Data Files in the Select XML Source dialog box, click EX N-3.xsd, click Open, then click OK**

   The schema elements appear in the XML Source task pane. Elements in a schema describe data similarly to the way field names in an Excel table describe the data in their columns. You choose the schema elements from the XML Source pane with which you want to work on your worksheet and map them to the worksheet. Once on the worksheet, the elements are called fields.

4. **Click the BRANCH element in the XML Source task pane and drag it to cell A1 on the worksheet, then use FIGURE N-12 as a guide to drag the FNAME, LNAME, SALES, and ENUMBER fields to the worksheet**

   The mapped elements appear in bolded format in the XML Source pane. The fields on the worksheet have filter arrows because Excel automatically creates a table on the worksheet as you map the schema elements. You decide to remove the ENUMBER field from the table.

5. **Right-click the ENUMBER element in the XML Source task pane, then click Remove element**

   ENUMBER is no longer formatted in bold because it is no longer mapped to the worksheet. This means that when XML data is imported, the ENUMBER field will not be populated with data. However, the field name remains in the table on the worksheet.

6. **Drag the table resizing arrow to the left to remove cell E1 from the table**

   Because you plan to import XML data from different files, you want to be sure that data from one file will not overwrite data from another file when it is imported into the worksheet. You also want to be sure that Excel validates the imported data against the rules specified in the schema.

7. **Click any cell in the table, click the DEVELOPER tab, then click the Map Properties button in the XML group**

   The XML Map Properties dialog box opens, as shown in **FIGURE N-13**.

8. **Click the Validate data against schema for import and export check box to select it, click the Append new data to existing XML tables option button to select it, then click OK**

   You are ready to import XML data into your worksheet.

FIGURE N-11: XML Maps dialog box

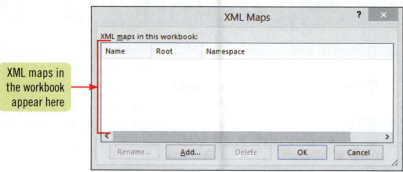

XML maps in the workbook appear here

FIGURE N-12: XML elements mapped to the worksheet

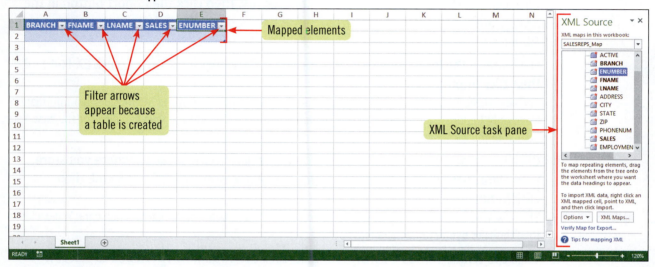

Mapped elements

Filter arrows appear because a table is created

XML Source task pane

FIGURE N-13: XML Map Properties dialog box

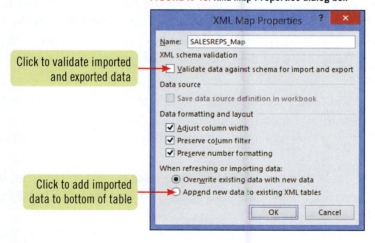

Click to validate imported and exported data

Click to add imported data to bottom of table

Learning more about XML

XML is a universal data format for business and industry information sharing. Using XML, you can store structured information related to services, products, or business transactions and easily share and exchange the information with others. XML provides a way to express structure in data. Structured data is tagged, or marked up, to indicate its content. For example, an XML data marker (tag) that contains an item's cost might be named COST. The ability of Excel to work with XML data lets you access the large amount of information stored in the XML format. For example, organizations have developed many XML applications with a specific focus, such as MathML (Mathematical Markup Language) and RETML (Real Estate Transaction Markup Language).

Import and Export XML Data

Learning Outcomes
• Import XML data into a workbook
• Export Excel data into an XML file

After the mapping is complete, you can import any XML file with a structure that conforms to the workbook schema. The mapped elements on the worksheet will fill with (or be **populated** with) data from the XML file. If an element is not mapped on the worksheet, then its data will not be imported. Once you import the XML data, you can analyze it using Excel tools. You can also export data from an Excel workbook to an XML file. **CASE** *Kate asks you to combine the sales data for the Miami and New York branches that are contained in XML files. She would like you to add a total for the combined branches and export the data from Excel to an XML file.*

STEPS

1. **Click cell A1, click the DEVELOPER tab if necessary, then click the Import button in the XML group**

   The Import XML dialog box opens.

2. **Navigate to the location where you store your Data Files if necessary, click EX N-4.xml, then click Import**

   The worksheet is populated with data from the XML file that contains the Miami sales rep information. Excel only imports data for the mapped elements. You decide to add the sales rep data for the New York branch to the worksheet.

3. **Click the Import button in the XML group, navigate to the location where you store your Data Files in the Import XML dialog box if necessary, click EX N-5.xml, then click Import**

   The New York branch sales rep data is added to the worksheet, below the Miami branch data. You decide to total the sales figures for all sales reps.

4. **Click the TABLE TOOLS DESIGN tab, then click the Total Row check box to select it**

   The total sales amount of 4974777 appears in cell D25. You decide to format the table.

5. **Select the range D2:D25, click the HOME tab, click the Accounting Number Format button $ in the Number group, click the Decrease Decimal button in the Number group twice, click the TABLE TOOLS DESIGN tab, click the More button in the Table Styles group, select Table Style Light 14, then click cell A1**

   Compare your completed table to **FIGURE N-14**.

6. **Enter your name in the center section of the worksheet footer, then preview the table**

   You will export the combined sales rep data as an XML file. Because not all of the elements in the schema were mapped to fields in your Excel table, you do not want the data exported from the table to be validated against the schema.

7. **Click any cell in the table, click the DEVELOPER tab, click the Map Properties button in the XML group, then click the Validate data against schema for import and export check box to deselect it**

   The Map Properties dialog box with the validation turned off is shown in **FIGURE N-15**. You are ready to export the XML data.

8. **Click OK, click the Export button in the XML group, navigate to the location where you store your Data Files in the Export XML dialog box, enter the name EX N-East Reps in the File name text box, click Export, then save and close the workbook**

   The sales data is saved in your Data File location in XML format, in the file called EX N-East Reps.xml.

FIGURE N-14: Completed table with combined sales rep data

Imported data is formatted →

Total sales ←

FIGURE N-15: XML Map Properties dialog box

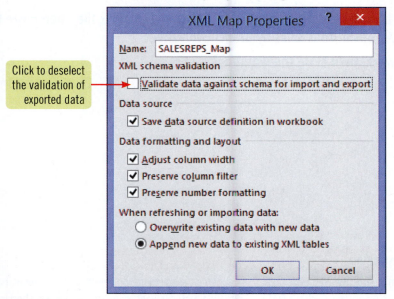

Click to deselect the validation of exported data →

Importing XML data without a schema

You can import XML data without a schema, and Excel will create one for you. In this situation all of the XML elements are mapped to the Excel worksheet, and the data in all of the fields is populated using the XML file. When a schema is not used, you are unable to validate the data that is imported. You also need to delete all of the fields in the table that you will not use in the worksheet, which can be time consuming.

Share Web Links

Learning Outcomes
• Save a workbook on a SkyDrive
• Copy a workbook web link

Often you'll want to share your Excel workbooks with co-workers. You can do this by sending them a link to your workbook. When you send a link to your workbook that is saved on your Sky Drive, your co-workers can use the Excel Web App to work with your file in the cloud. When you create the link, you can allow users to view the workbook, or to view and edit it. **CASE** ▶ *Kate is working on the sales results with the branch managers. She asks you to save the sales information in the cloud and give her a link that she can share with the managers.*

STEPS

1. **Open the file EX N-1.xlsx from the location where you store your Data Files, then save it as EX N-Tour Sales**

   You need to save the file to your Sky Drive account before you can send a link to it.

2. **Click the FILE tab, click Share, then click Invite People if necessary**

   The Share window opens, showing the steps to invite people to use your workbook as shown in **FIGURE N-16**.

3. **Click Save To Cloud, click Save As if necessary, navigate to your Sky Drive location, then click Save in the Save As dialog box**

4. **Click Get a Sharing Link**

   You will see more options in the Share window as shown in **FIGURE N-17**. You can choose to get a **View Link** which allows people to view your Excel file, or you can select an **Edit Link** which allows people to edit the file. You decide to create a View Link.

QUICK TIP
After you save a workbook on your SkyDrive, you can invite people to view or edit it in the cloud: Click the FILE tab, click Share, click Invite People, enter their email addresses, select the editing option, then click Share.

5. **Click the Create Link button next to the View Link, then copy the View Link URL**

   You decide to test the web link address by pasting it in your browser.

6. **Open your browser, paste the View Link URL in the address text box, then press [Enter]**

   The workbook opens in the Excel WebApp as shown in **FIGURE N-18**.

7. **Close your browser, return to the Excel EX N-Tour Sales.xlsx file, then paste the copied link in cell A7 of the Tour Sales by Branch worksheet**

8. **Save your work, then close the workbook**

Creating your own Web queries

The easiest way to retrieve data from a particular Web page on a regular basis is to create a customized Web query. Click the DATA tab, click the From Web button in the Get External Data group (or click the Get External Data button and click the From Web button). In the Address text box in the New Web Query dialog box, type the address of the Web page from which you want to retrieve data, then click Go. Click the yellow arrows next to the information you want to bring into a worksheet or click the upper-left arrow to import the entire page, verify that the information that you want to import has a green checkmark next to it, then click Import. The Import Data dialog box opens and allows you to specify where you want the imported data to appear in the worksheet or workbook. You can save a query for future use by clicking the Save Query button 🖫 in the New Web Query dialog box before you click Import. The query is saved as a file with an .iqy file extension.

Sharing Excel Files and Incorporating Web Information

FIGURE N-16: Share window with invite options

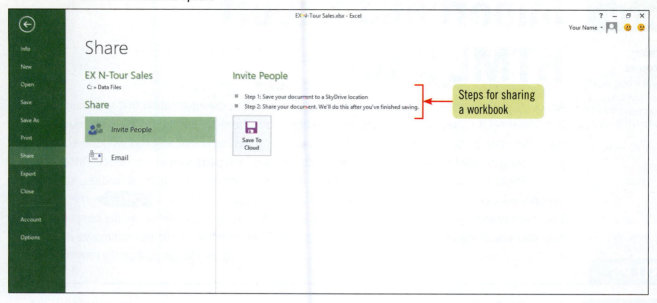

FIGURE N-17: Share window with link options

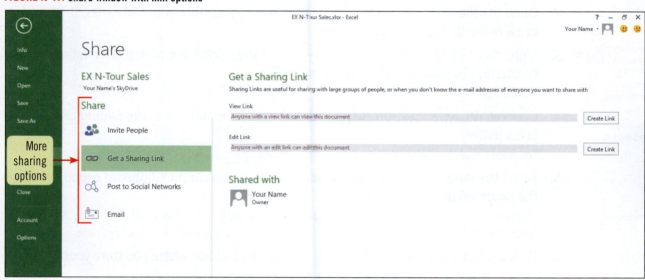

FIGURE N-18: Workbook in the Excel Web App

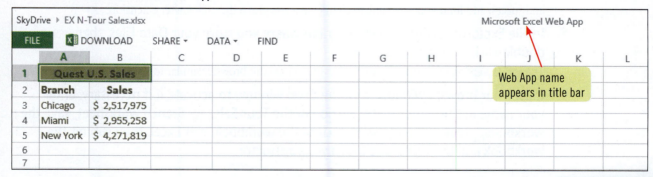

Import and Export HTML Data

Learning Outcomes
- Import HTML data into a workbook
- Export Excel data into an HTML file

Although you can open HTML files directly in Excel, most often the information that you want to include in a worksheet is published on the Web and you don't have the HTML file. In this situation you can import the HTML data by copying the data on the Web page and pasting it into an Excel worksheet. This allows you to bring in only the information that you need from the Web page to your worksheet. Once the HTML data is in your worksheet, you can analyze the imported information using Excel features. You can also export worksheet data as an HTML file that you can then share on a Web site. **CASE** *The Toronto and Vancouver branch managers have published the Canada branch sales information on the company intranet. Kate asks you to import the published sales data into an Excel worksheet so she can summarize it using Excel tools. She also wants you to export the summarized data to an HTML file she can post on the company intranet.*

STEPS

QUICK TIP
You need to use Internet Explorer as your browser for this lesson.

1. **In File Explorer, navigate to the location where you store your Data Files, double-click the file EX N-6.htm to open it in your browser, then copy the two table rows on the Web page containing the Toronto and Vancouver sales information**

   You are ready to paste the information from the Web page into an Excel worksheet.

2. **Open the file EX N-1.xlsx from the location where you store your Data Files, then save it as EX N-North America Sales**

TROUBLE
Pasting the data doesn't match all of the destination formats. You will fix the formatting of the pasted data in Step 5.

3. **Right-click cell A6 on the Tour Sales by Branch sheet, click the Match Destination Formatting button 📋 in the Paste Options list**

   The Canada sales information is added to the U.S. sales data.

4. **Click cell A8, type Total, press [Tab], click the AutoSum button in the Editing group, then press [Enter]**

   You want the font to be uniform throughout the worksheet.

5. **Select the range A5:B5, click the Format Painter button in the Clipboard group, select the range A6:B8, then click cell A1**

   Compare your worksheet to **FIGURE N-19**. Kate is finished with the analysis and formatting of the North America branches. She wants the combined worksheet information published in a Web page.

6. **Click the FILE tab, click Save As, then browse to the location where you store your Data Files**

   The Save As dialog box lets you specify what workbook parts you want to publish.

7. **Click the Save as type list arrow, click Web Page (*.htm;*.html), edit the filename to read nasales.htm, click the Selection: Sheet option button, click Publish, then click Publish again**

   The HTML file, containing only the tour Sales by Branch worksheet, is saved in your Data Files location. To avoid problems when publishing pages to a Web server, use lowercase characters, omit special characters and spaces, and limit your filename to eight characters plus a three-character extension.

8. **In File Explorer, navigate to the location where you store your Data Files, then double-click the file nasales.htm**

   The HTML version of your worksheet opens in your default browser, similar to **FIGURE N-20**.

9. **Close your browser window, click the Excel window to activate it if necessary, enter your name in the center footer section of the Tour Sales by Branch worksheet, save the workbook, preview the worksheet, close the workbook, exit Excel, then submit the workbook and the Web page file to your instructor**

FIGURE N-19: Worksheet with North America sales data

Formatted table with data added from HTML file

Two added rows

FIGURE N-20: North America Sales as Web page

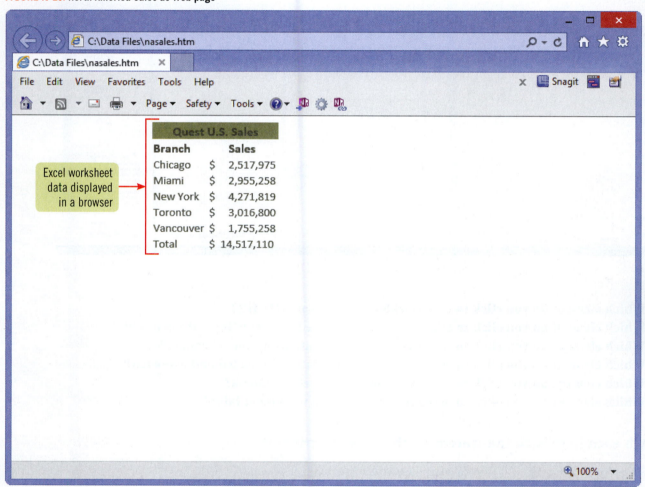

Excel worksheet data displayed in a browser

Adding Web hyperlinks to a worksheet

In Excel worksheets, you can create hyperlinks to information on the Web. Every Web page is identified by a unique Web address called a Uniform Resource Locator (URL). To create a hyperlink to a Web page, click the cell for which you want to create a hyperlink, click the INSERT tab, click the Hyperlink button in the Links group, under Link to: make sure Existing File or Web Page is selected, specify the target for the hyperlink (the URL) in the Address text box, then click OK. If there is text in the cell, the text format changes to become a blue underlined hyperlink or the color the current workbook theme uses for hyperlinks. If there is no text in the cell, the Web site's URL appears in the cell.

Sharing Excel Files and Incorporating Web Information

Practice

Concepts Review

FIGURE N-21

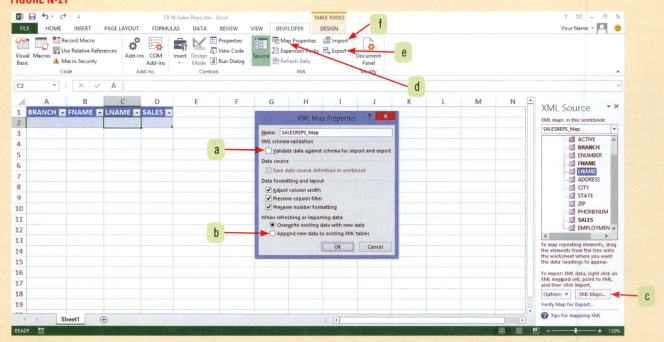

1. Which element do you click to save workbook data to an XML file?
2. Which element do you click to add imported XML data below existing data in a table?
3. Which element do you click to check imported XML data using the schema rules?
4. Which element do you click to change the way XML data is imported and exported?
5. Which element do you click to add a schema to an Excel workbook?
6. Which element do you click to bring in XML data to a workbook table?

Match each item with the statement that best describes it.

7. Password
8. Change history
9. Shared workbook
10. xsd
11. iqy

a. The file extension for an XML schema
b. A record of edits others have made to a worksheet
c. Used to protect a workbook from unauthorized use
d. The file extension for a Web query
e. A file used by many people on a network

Select the best answer from the list of choices.

12. Which of the following is the best example of a strong password for a workbook?
    a. myfile
    b. MollY
    c. MYFILE
    d. my%File95gz

13. Which of the following sharing links allows people to make changes to your Excel data?
    a. Change Link
    b. Edit Link
    c. View Link
    d. Import Link

14. The process of selecting XML elements to include on a worksheet is called:
    a. Sharing.
    b. Selecting.
    c. Mapping.
    d. Loading.

15. A file that describes the structure of XML data is called a:
    a. Query.
    b. Schema.
    c. Layout.
    d. Detail File.

Skills Review

1. **Set up a shared workbook for multiple users.**
   a. Start Excel, open the file EX N-7.xlsx from the location where you store your Data Files, then save it as **EX N-Sales**.
   b. Use the Share Workbook command on the REVIEW tab to set up the workbook so that more than one person can use it at one time.
   c. Save the workbook when asked to save it.
   d. Verify the workbook is marked as Shared in the title bar.
   e. Review the regional sales data for the first two quarters of the year.

2. **Track revisions in a shared workbook.**
   a. Change the Seattle sales to **$50,000** for the first quarter and **$45,000** for the second quarter.
   b. Save the file.
   c. Display the History sheet by opening the Highlight Changes dialog box, deselecting the When check box, then selecting the option for List changes on a new sheet.
   d. Compare your History sheet to **FIGURE N-22**.
   e. Copy the range A1:I3 in the History sheet, add a new worksheet and paste the range in the new worksheet. Widen the columns to display all of the information, then rename the new worksheet to **History Sheet**.

   FIGURE N-22

	A	B	C	D	E	F	G	H	I	J	K	L
1	Action Number	Date	Time	Who	Change	Sheet	Range	New Value	Old Value	Action Type	Losing Action	
2	1	12/3/2016	2:38 PM	Your Name	Cell Change	Sales	C2	$50,000.00	$32,988.00			
3	2	12/3/2016	2:38 PM	Your Name	Cell Change	Sales	D2	$45,000.00	$28,364.00			
4												
5	The history ends with the changes saved on 12/3/2016 at 2:38 PM.											
6												

   f. Enter your name in the History Sheet footer, then preview the History Sheet.
   g. Save the workbook, close it, then submit the workbook to your instructor.

3. **Apply and modify passwords.**
   a. Open the file EX N-7.xlsx from the location where you store your Data Files, open the Save As dialog box, then open the General Options dialog box.
   b. Set the password to open the workbook as **Sales11** and the password to modify it as **FirstHalf11**.
   c. Save the password-protected file as **EX N-Sales PW** in the location where you store your Data Files.
   d. Close the workbook.
   e. Use the assigned passwords to reopen the workbook and verify that you can change it by adding your name in the center section of the Sales sheet footer, save the workbook, preview the Sales worksheet, close the workbook, then submit the workbook to your instructor.

Excel 2013

Skills Review (continued)

4. Work with XML schemas.

a. Open a new blank workbook, then save it as **EX N-Contact Information** in the location where you store your Data Files.

b. Open the XML Source pane, and add the XML schema EX N-8.xsd to the workbook.

c. Map the FNAME element to cell A1 on the worksheet, LNAME to cell B1, PHONENUM to cell C1, and EMPLOYMENT_DATE to cell D1.

d. Remove the EMPLOYMENT_DATE element from the map, and delete the field from the table.

e. Use the XML Map Properties dialog box to make sure imported XML data is validated using the schema.

5. Import and export XML data.

a. Import the XML file EX N-9.xml into the workbook.

b. Sort the worksheet list in ascending order by LNAME.

c. Add the Table Style Light 13 to the table, and compare your screen to **FIGURE N-23**.

d. Enter your name in the center section of the worksheet footer, save the workbook, then preview the worksheet.

e. Use the XML Map Properties dialog box to turn off the validation for imported and exported worksheet data, export the worksheet data to an XML file named **EX N-Contact**, save and close the workbook.

FIGURE N-23

	A	B	C
1	FNAME	LNAME	PHONENUM
2	Kathy	Conolly	503-302-1163
3	Jack	Green	503-367-4156
4	Elaine	Jackson	503-392-8163
5	Linda	MacNeal	503-932-9966
6	Kelly	Maguire	503-272-9456
7	Kris	Malone	503-722-9163
8	Bruce	Nangle	503-322-3163
9	Meg	Shelly	503-322-3163
10			

6. Share Web Links.

a. Open the file EX N-7.xlsx from the location where you store your Data Files, then save it as **EX N-Region Sales**.

b. Save the EX-Region Sales file to your SkyDrive.

c. Enter **View Link** in cell A24. Get a sharing link that allows the recipient to view the workbook. Paste the link in cell B24.

d. Enter **Edit Link** in cell A25. Get a sharing link that allows the recipient to edit the workbook. Paste the link in cell B25.

e. Compare your screen to **FIGURE N-24**. (Your links will be different.)

f. Change the page orientation to landscape, enter your name in the center section of the worksheet header, preview the worksheet, then save the workbook in the location where you store your Data Files.

FIGURE N-24

	A	B	C	D	E	F	G	H
16	South	Tampa	$17,662	$21,854				
17	South	Dallas	$16,557	$19,633				
18	South	San Diego	$19,551	$16,855				
19	South	Santa Fe	$25,448	$42,887				
20	South	Charlotte	$21,662	$21,996				
21	South	Biloxi	$20,335	$16,833				
22	South	Houston	$25,700	$17,627				
23								
24	View Link	https://skydrive.live.com/redir?page=view&resid=123456789!123&authkey=!QWTYU075P						
25	Edit Link	https://skydrive.live.com/redir?page=view&resid=123456789!123&authkey=!ABZS147B87						
26								

g. Close the workbook, and submit the workbook to your instructor.

7. Import and export HTML data.

a. Open the file EX N-7.xlsx from the location where you store your Data Files, then save it as **EX N-Sales2**.

b. Open the file EX N-10.htm in your browser from the location where you store your Data Files. Copy the data in the four rows of the Web page (not the column headings), and paste it below the data in the Sales sheet of the EX N-Sales2 workbook.

c. On the Sales sheet, enter **Total** in cell A27, and use **AutoSum** in cells C27 and D27 to total the values in columns C and D.

Skills Review (continued)

    d. Adjust the formatting for the new rows to match the other rows on the Sales sheet, add your name to the center section of the worksheet footer, save the workbook, then preview the Sales sheet.

    e. Save the data on the Sales sheet as an HTML file with the name **sales2.htm**.

    f. Close the workbook, exit Excel, open the sales2.htm file in your browser, compare your screen to **FIGURE N-25**, close your browser, then submit the sales2.htm file to your instructor.

Independent Challenge 1

You are the registrar at West End College. One of your responsibilities is to work with the school's Academic Dean on the course schedule. You use shared Excel workbooks to help you with this scheduling by sharing the workbook with your first draft schedule with the Dean. You have received the shared workbook from the Dean with her changes that include location edits and you will review the workbooks and accept the changes which have your approval.

    a. Start Excel, open the file EX N-11.xlsx from the location where you store your Data Files, then save it as **EX N-Fall Quarter**.

    b. Use the Accept or Reject dialog box to accept the first three changes and reject the fourth change to the workbook.

    c. Use the Highlight Changes dialog box to highlight the change on the screen. Review the ScreenTip details.

    d. Use the Highlight Changes dialog box to create a History worksheet detailing the changes to the workbook.

    e. Copy the information about the change in the range A1:I5, and paste it in a new worksheet.

    f. Widen the columns as necessary, and rename the new sheet **History Sheet**. Compare your History Sheet to **FIGURE N-26**.

    g. Add your name to the center section of the History sheet footer, then preview the History worksheet.

    h. Remove the Shared status of the workbook. (*Hint*: In the Share Workbook dialog box, deselect the "Allow changes by more than one user at the same time." checkbox.)

    i. Add a password of **Fall%2016** to open the workbook and **Courses%2016** to modify it.

    j. Save and close the workbook. Submit the EX N-Fall Quarter.xlsx workbook to your instructor.

FIGURE N-25

Region	Store	Quarter 1	Quarter 2
North	Seattle	$32,988	$28,364
North	Portland	$29,302	$25,100
North	Minneapolis	$31,805	$21,601
North	Madison	$32,669	$22,471
North	Billings	$30,410	$25,445
North	Columbus	$32,577	$21,877
North	Boston	$42,358	$26,647
North	Hartford	$31,633	$22,541
North	Concord	$30,000	$32,145
North	New York	$18,521	$32,451
North	Newark	$16,201	$29,365
North	San Francisco	$19,105	$20,100
South	Miami	$17,511	$23,654
South	New Orleans	$14,652	$29,654
South	Tampa	$17,662	$21,854
South	Dallas	$16,557	$19,633
South	San Diego	$19,551	$16,855
South	Santa Fe	$25,448	$42,887
South	Charlotte	$21,662	$21,996
South	Biloxi	$20,335	$16,833
South	Houston	$25,700	$17,627
West	Los Angeles	$34,675	$46,789
West	Las Vegas	$37,175	$47,119
West	Denver	$34,175	$57,841
West	Salt Lake	$31,024	$45,127
Total		$663,696	$715,976

FIGURE N-26

	A	B	C	D	E	F	G	H	I
1	Action Number	Date	Time	Who	Change	Sheet	Range	New Value	Old Value
2	1	12/3/2016	3:39 PM	Maria Gonzalez	Cell Change	Fall Semester	F2	N102	N122
3	2	12/3/2016	3:39 PM	Maria Gonzalez	Cell Change	Fall Semester	F5	S210	S214
4	3	12/3/2016	3:39 PM	Maria Gonzalez	Cell Change	Fall Semester	F8	N100	N101
5	4	12/3/2016	3:39 PM	Maria Gonzalez	Cell Change	Fall Semester	F13	S217	S215
6									

Independent Challenge 2

The North Shore Health Club is a fitness center with five fitness facilities. As the general manager you are responsible for setting and publishing the membership rate information. You decide to run a special promotion offering a 10 percent discount off the current membership prices. You will also add two new membership categories to help attract younger members. The membership rate information is published on the company Web site. You will copy the rate information from the Web page and work with it in Excel to calculate the special discounted rates. You will save the new rate information as an HTML file so it can be published on the Web.

Independent Challenge 2 (continued)

a. Open the file EX N-12.htm from the location where you store your Data Files to display it in your browser.

b. Start Excel, create a new workbook, then save it as **EX N-Rates** in the location where you store your Data Files.

c. Return to the browser, copy the five rows of data, including the column headings from the table in the EX N-12 file, and paste them in the EX N-Rates workbook. Adjust the column widths as necessary. Close the EX N-12.htm file.

d. Add the new membership data from the table below in rows 6 and 7 of the worksheet.

Membership	Price
Teen	250
Youth	175

e. Remove the borders around the cells in columns A and B. (*Hint*: Select the range A1:B7, click the Border list arrow, then click No Border.)

f. Enter **Special** in cell C1, and calculate each special rate in column C by discounting the prices in column B by 10%. (*Hint*: Multiply each price by .90.)

g. Format the price information in columns B and C with the Accounting format using the $ symbol with two decimal places. Widen the columns as necessary.

h. Add the passwords **Members11** to open the EX N-Rates workbook and **Gym11** to modify it. Save the workbook, replacing the existing file, close the workbook, then reopen it by entering the passwords.

i. Verify that you can modify the workbook by formatting the worksheet using the Office Theme font color Green, Accent 6, Darker 50%.

j. Format the label in cell C1 as bold. Compare your worksheet data to **FIGURE N-27**.

k. Add your name to the center footer section of the worksheet, save the workbook, then preview the worksheet.

l. Save the worksheet data in HTML format using the name **prices.htm**. Close the workbook and exit Excel.

m. Open the prices.htm page in your browser and print the page.

n. Close your browser. Submit the prices.htm and the EX N-Rates file to your instructor.

FIGURE N-27

	A	B	C
1	Membership	Price	Special
2	Family	$875.00	$787.50
3	Adult	$675.00	$607.50
4	Senior	$275.00	$247.50
5	College	$280.00	$252.00
6	Teen	$250.00	$225.00
7	Youth	$175.00	$157.50
8			

Independent Challenge 3

You are the director of development at a local hospital. You are preparing the phone lists for your annual fundraising event. The donor information for the organization is in an XML file, which you will bring into Excel to organize. You will use an XML schema to map only the donors' names and phone numbers to the worksheet. This will allow you to import the donor data and limit the information that is distributed to the phone-a-thon volunteers. You will also import information about the donors from another XML file. You will export your worksheet data as XML for future use.

a. Start Excel, create a new workbook, then save it as **EX N-Donors** in the location where you store your Data Files.

b. Add the map EX N-13.xsd from the location where you store your Data Files to the workbook.

c. Map the FNAME element to cell A1, LNAME to cell B1, and PHONENUM to cell C1. Make sure that imported XML data will be validated using the schema rules.

d. Import the XML data in file EX N-14.xml from the location where you store your Data Files. Add the Table Style Light 20 to the table. Change the field name in cell A1 to **FIRST NAME**, change the field name in cell B1 to **LAST NAME**, and change the field name in cell C1 to **PHONE NUMBER**. Widen the columns as necessary to accommodate the full field names.

Independent Challenge 3 (continued)

e. Sort the table in ascending order by LAST NAME. Compare your sorted table to **FIGURE N-28**.

f. Open the XML Map Properties dialog box to verify the Overwrite existing data with new data option button is selected. Map the ACTIVE element to cell D1. Import the XML data in file EX N-14.xml again.

g. Map the CONTRIB_DATE element to cell E1. Import the XML data in file EX N-14.xml a third time. Change the field name in cell E1 to **LAST DONATION**, and widen the column to accommodate the full field name.

h. Filter the table to show only active donors. Compare your filtered table to **FIGURE N-29**.

i. Export the worksheet data to an XML file named **EX N-Phone List**.

j. Enter your name in the center section of the worksheet footer, preview the worksheet in landscape orientation, then save the workbook.

k. Close the workbook, exit Excel, then submit the workbook and the XML file to your instructor.

FIGURE N-28

	A	B	C
1	FIRST NAME ▼	LAST NAME ⏷	PHONE NUMBER ▼
2	Peg	Allen	312-765-8756
3	Ellen	Atkins	773-167-4156
4	Kathy	Breen	773-220-9456
5	Sally	Colby	312-322-3163
6	Betty	Daly	312-322-3163
7	Ken	Gonzales	773-379-0092
8	Julio	Herandez	312-765-8756
9	Ann	Land	312-299-4298
10	Lynn	Neal	312-932-9966
11	Mark	Zoll	312-765-8756
12			

FIGURE N-29

	A	B	C	D	E
1	FIRST NAME ▼	LAST NAME ⏷	PHONE NUMBER ▼	ACTIVE ⏷	LAST DONATION ▼
2	Kathy	Breen	773-220-9456	TRUE	Jan-15
4	Lynn	Neal	312-932-9966	TRUE	Jan-14
7	Ken	Gonzales	773-379-0092	TRUE	Nov-14
9	Mark	Zoll	312-765-8756	TRUE	Dec-13
10	Peg	Allen	312-765-8756	TRUE	Nov-12
11	Julio	Herandez	312-765-8756	TRUE	Dec-13
12					

Independent Challenge 4: Explore

You will explore the Apps for Office available to use in worksheets and share your results in the Cloud by inviting people to view your workbook saved on your SkyDrive.

a. Start Excel, create a new blank workbook, then save it as **EX N-WebApp** in the location where you store your Data Files.

b. View the featured apps for Office. (*Hint*: Click the INSERT tab, click the Apps for Office button in the Apps group, then click FEATURED APPS at the top of the window if necessary.)

c. Insert a free app from the Featured Apps collection.

d. Explore the app to develop an understanding of its purpose.

e. If you have data in rows one, two, or three from your app, insert three rows above the data. In cell A1 of your worksheet, enter App Name. Enter the name of your app in cell B1.

f. In rows 2 and 3 of the worksheet enter information about the purpose of the app.

g. Enter your name in the center section of the worksheet footer.

h. Save your EX N-WebApp workbook on your SkyDrive.

i. Share your EX N-WebApp workbook by inviting a classmate to view it. If you don't have a classmate's email address you can use your own email address. (*Hint*: Click the FILE tab, click Share, click Invite People, enter the email address, click the Can edit list arrow, select Can view, then click Share.)

j. Get sharing links to view the workbook and to edit the workbook.

k. Create a new worksheet, name the worksheet Links, then copy the sharing links and paste them into the new worksheet with labels identifying each one.

l. Save the workbook to the location where you store your Data Files replacing the previously saved workbook.

m. Close the workbook, exit Excel, then submit the workbook to your instructor.

Visual Workshop

Start Excel, create a new workbook, then save it as **EX N-Shore.xlsx** in the location where you store your Data Files. Open the file EX N-15.htm in your browser from the location where you store your Data Files. Create the worksheet shown in **FIGURE N-30** by pasting the information from the Web page into your EX N-Shore.xlsx file, formatting it, adding the fourth quarter information, adding the totals, and replacing Your Name with your name. (*Hint*: The colors are in the Office theme, the font size of the first three rows is 14 and the remaining font size is 12.) Add your name to the footer of Sheet1, preview the worksheet, then save the workbook. Submit the EX N-Shore.xlsx workbook to your instructor.

FIGURE N-30

	A	B	C	D	E	F
1	Shore Catering					
2	Sales Report					
3	Your Name					
4	Category	1st Quarter	2nd Quarter	3rd Quarter	4th Quarter	Totals
5	Corporate	$ 13,267	$ 11,345	$ 12,212	$ 11,542	$ 48,366
6	Weddings	$ 9,340	$ 11,876	$ 14,876	$ 15,247	$ 51,339
7	Home Celebrations	$ 7,023	$ 9,154	$ 9,423	$ 13,274	$ 38,874
8	Functions	$ 9,432	$ 9,331	$ 11,213	$ 10,284	$ 40,260
9	Delivery	$ 6,432	$ 5,331	$ 6,713	$ 21,874	$ 40,350
10	Totals	$ 45,494	$ 47,037	$ 54,437	$ 72,221	$ 219,189
11						

Customizing Excel and Advanced Worksheet Management

CASE ▶ Quest's vice president of sales, Kate Morgan, asks you to review sales worksheet formulas, customize Excel workbooks, and create a sales template. You will use Excel tools and options to help Kate and the sales staff work quickly and efficiently in a customized environment.

Unit Objectives

After completing this unit, you will be able to:

- Audit a worksheet
- Control worksheet calculations
- Group worksheet data
- Work with cell comments

- Create custom AutoFill lists
- Create and apply a template
- Customize Excel workbooks
- Customize the Excel screen

Files You Will Need

EX O-1.xlsx   EX O-5.xlsx
EX O-2.xlsx   EX O-6.xlsx
EX O-3.xlsx   EX O-7.xlsx
EX O-4.xlsx

©Katerina Havelkova/Shutterstock

Learning Outcomes
- Locate formula errors
- Correct formula errors

Audit a Worksheet

Because errors can occur at any stage of worksheet development, it is important to include auditing as part of your workbook-building process. The Excel **auditing** feature helps you track errors and check worksheet logic to make sure your worksheet is error free and the data is arranged sensibly. The Formula Auditing group on the FORMULAS tab contains several error-checking tools to help you audit a worksheet. **CASE** ▶ *Kate asks you to help identify errors in the worksheet that tracks sales for the two Canadian branches to verify the accuracy of year-end totals and percentages.*

STEPS

1. **Start Excel, open the file EX O-1.xlsx from the location where you store your Data Files, then save it as EX O-Canada Sales**

2. **Click the FORMULAS tab, then click the Error Checking button in the Formula Auditing group**

   The Error Checking dialog box opens and alerts you to a Divide by Zero Error in cell O5, as shown in **FIGURE O-1**. The formula reads =N5/N8, indicating that the value in cell N5 will be divided by the value in cell N8. In Excel formulas, blank cells have a value of zero. This error means the value in cell N5 cannot be divided by the value in cell N8 (zero) because division by zero is not mathematically possible. To correct the error, you must edit the formula so that it references cell N7, the total of sales, not cell N8.

3. **Click Edit in Formula Bar in the Error Checking dialog box, edit the formula in the formula bar to read =N5/N7, click the Enter button ☑, then click Resume in the Error Checking dialog box**

   The edited formula produces the correct result, .5547, in cell O5. The Error Checking dialog box indicates another error in cell N6, the total Vancouver sales. The formula reads =SUM(B6:L6) and should be =SUM(B6:M6). The top button in the Error Checking dialog box changes to "Copy Formula from Above". Since this formula in the cell N5 is correct, you will copy it.

4. **Click Copy Formula from Above**

   The Vancouver total changes to $318,130 in cell N6. The Error Checking dialog box finds another division-by-zero error in cell O6. You decide to use another tool in the Formula Auditing group to get more information about this error.

5. **Close the Error Checking dialog box, then click the Trace Precedents button in the Formula Auditing group**

   Blue arrows called **tracer arrows** point from the cells referenced by the formula to the active cell as shown in **FIGURE O-2**. The arrows help you determine if these cell references might have caused the error. The tracer arrows extend from the error to cells N6 and N8. To correct the error, you must edit the formula so that it references cell N7 in the denominator, the sales total, not cell N8.

6. **Edit the formula in the formula bar to read =N6/N7, then click ☑ on the formula bar**

   The result of the formula, .4453, appears in cell O6. The November sales for the Vancouver branch in cell L6 is unusually high compared with sales posted for the other months. You can investigate the other cells in the sheet that are affected by the value of cell L6 by tracing the cell's **dependents**—the cells that contain formulas referring to cell L6.

7. **Click cell L6, then click the Trace Dependents button in the Formula Auditing group**

   The tracer arrows run from cell L6 to cells L7 and N6, indicating that the value in cell L6 affects the total November sales and the total Vancouver sales. You decide to remove the tracer arrows and format the percentages in cells O5 and O6.

8. **Click the Remove Arrows button in the Formula Auditing group, select the range O5:O6, click the HOME tab, click the Percent Style button % in the Number group, click the Increase Decimal button ⇥.00 twice, return to cell A1, then save the workbook**

Customizing Excel and Advanced Worksheet Management

FIGURE O-1: Error Checking dialog box

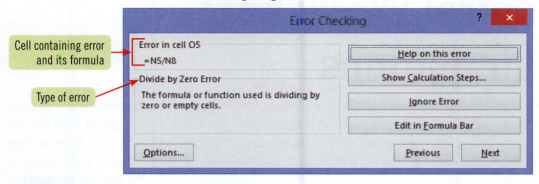

Cell containing error and its formula

Type of error

Error Checking

? ✕

Error in cell O5

= N5/N8

Divide by Zero Error

The formula or function used is dividing by zero or empty cells.

Help on this error

Show Calculation Steps...

Ignore Error

Edit in Formula Bar

Options...

Previous   Next

FIGURE O-2: Worksheet with traced error

	A	B	C	D	E	F	G	H	I	J	K	L	M	N	O
1							Quest Canada								
2							2016 Sales Summary								
3															
4	Branch	Jan	Feb	Mar	Apr	May	Jun	Jul	Aug	Sep	Oct	Nov	Dec	Total	Percent
5	Toronto	$37,348	$34,882	$37,842	$40,880	$14,232	$31,557	$30,790	$39,786	$32,992	$30,102	$34,022	$31,852	$396,285	0.5547
6	Vancouver	$25,698	$21,741	$26,349	$29,843	$31,791	$21,921	$20,941	$19,812	$27,341	$21,841	$51,711	$19,141	$318,130	#DIV/0!
7	Total	$63,046	$56,623	$64,191	$70,723	$46,023	$53,478	$51,731	$59,598	$60,333	$51,943	$85,733	$50,993	$714,415	
8															

Tracer arrows

Watching and evaluating formulas

As you edit your worksheet, you can watch the effect that cell changes have on selected worksheet formulas. Select the cell or cells that you want to watch, click the FORMULAS tab, click the Watch Window button in the Formula Auditing group, click Add Watch in the Watch Window, then click Add. The Watch Window displays the workbook name, worksheet name, the cell address you want to watch, the current cell value, and its formula. As cell values that "feed into" the formula change, the resulting formula value in the Watch Window changes. To delete a watch, select the cell information in the Watch Window, then click Delete Watch. You can also step through a formula, and its results: Select a cell that contains a formula, then click the Evaluate Formula button in the Formula Auditing group. The formula appears in the Evaluation Window of the Evaluate Formula dialog box. As you click the Evaluate button, the cell references are replaced with their values and the formula result.

Control Worksheet Calculations

Whenever you change a value in a cell, Excel automatically recalculates all the formulas in the worksheet based on that cell. This automatic calculation is efficient until you create a worksheet so large that the recalculation process slows down data entry and screen updating. Worksheets with many formulas, data tables, or functions may also recalculate slowly. In these cases, you might want to selectively determine if and when you want Excel to perform calculations. You do this by applying the **manual calculation** option. Once you change the calculation mode to manual, Excel applies manual calculation to all open worksheets. **CASE** *Because Kate knows that using specific Excel calculation options can help make worksheet building more efficient, she asks you to review the formula settings in the workbook and change the formula calculations from automatic to manual calculation.*

STEPS

1. **Click the FILE tab, click Options, then click Formulas in the list of options**
    The options related to formula calculation and error checking appear, as shown in **FIGURE O-3**.

2. **Under Calculation options, click to select the Manual option button**
    When you select the Manual option, the Recalculate workbook before saving check box automatically becomes active and contains a check mark. Because the workbook will not recalculate until you save or close and reopen the workbook, you must make sure to recalculate your worksheet before you print it and after you finish making changes.

3. **Click OK**
    Kate informs you that the December total for the Toronto branch is incorrect. You adjust the entry in cell M5 to reflect the actual sales figure.

4. **Click cell M5**
    Before changing cell M5, notice that in cell N5 the total for the Toronto branch is $396,285, and the Toronto percent in cell O5 is 55.47%.

5. **Type 40,000, then click the Enter button ☑ on the formula bar**
    The total and percent formulas are *not* updated. The total in cell N5 is still $396,285 and the percentage in cell O5 is still 55.47%. The word "Calculate" appears in the status bar to indicate that a specific value in the worksheet did indeed change and that the worksheet must be recalculated.

6. **Click the FORMULAS tab, click the Calculate Sheet button in the Calculation group, click cell A1, then save the workbook**
    The total in cell N5 is now $404,433 instead of $396,285 and the percentage in cell O5 is now 55.97% instead of 55.47%. The other formulas in the worksheet affected by the value in cell M5 changed as well, as shown in **FIGURE O-4**. Because this is a relatively small worksheet that recalculates quickly, you will return to automatic calculation.

7. **Click the Calculations Options button in the Calculation group, then click Automatic**
    Now any additional changes you make will automatically recalculate the worksheet formulas.

8. **Place your name in the center section of the worksheet footer, then save the workbook**

FIGURE O-3: Excel formula options

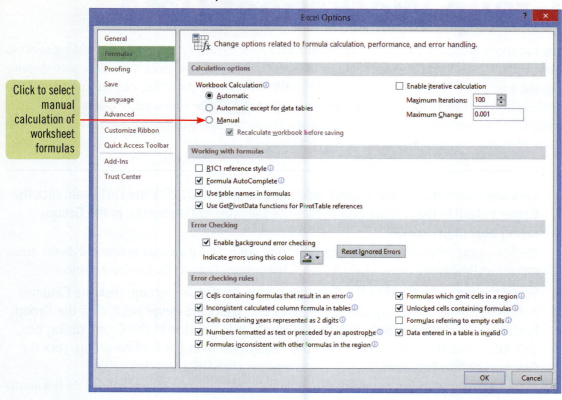

Click to select manual calculation of worksheet formulas

FIGURE O-4: Worksheet with updated values

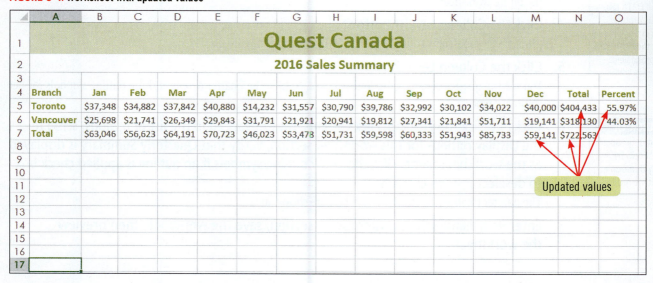

Updated values

Group Worksheet Data

Learning Outcomes
• Group worksheet data
• Outline worksheet data

You can create groups of rows and columns on a worksheet to manage your data and make it easier to work with. The Excel grouping feature provides an outline with symbols that allow you to easily expand and collapse groups to show or hide selected worksheet data. You can turn off the outline symbols if you are using the condensed data in a report. **CASE** ▶ *Kate needs to give Jessica Long, the Quest CEO, the quarterly sales totals for the Canadian branches. She asks you to group the worksheet data by quarters.*

STEPS

1. **Click the Quarterly Summary sheet, select the range B4:D7, click the DATA tab, click the Group button in the Outline group, click the Columns option button in the Group dialog box, then click OK**

   The first quarter information is grouped, and **outline symbols** that are used to hide and display details appear over the columns, as shown in **FIGURE O-5**. You continue to group the remaining quarters.

2. **Select the range F4:H7, click the Group button in the Outline group, click the Columns option button in the Group dialog box, click OK, select the range J4:L7, click the Group button in the Outline group, click the Columns option button in the Group dialog box, click OK, select the range N4:P7, click the Group button in the Outline group, click the Columns option button in the Group dialog box, click OK, then click cell A1**

   All four quarters are grouped. You decide to use the outline symbols to expand and collapse the first quarter information.

3. **Click the Collapse Outline button ⊟ above the column E label, then click the Expand Outline button ⊞ above the column E label**

   Clicking the (−) symbol temporarily hides the Q1 detail columns, and the (−) symbol changes to a (+) symbol. Clicking the (+) symbol expands the Q1 details and redisplays the hidden columns. The Column Level symbols in the upper-left corner of the worksheet are used to display and hide levels of detail across the entire worksheet.

4. **Click the Column Level 1 button ①**

   All of the group details collapse, and only the quarter totals are displayed.

5. **Click the Column Level 2 button ②**

   You see the quarter details again. Kate asks you to hide the quarter details and the outline symbols for her summary report.

6. **Click ①, click the FILE tab, click Options, click Advanced in the list of options, scroll to the Display options for this worksheet section, verify that Quarterly Summary is displayed as the worksheet name, click the Show outline symbols if an outline is applied check box to deselect it, then click OK**

   The quarter totals without outline symbols are shown in **FIGURE O-6**.

7. **Enter your name in the center footer section, save the workbook, then preview the worksheet**

FIGURE O-5: First quarter data grouped

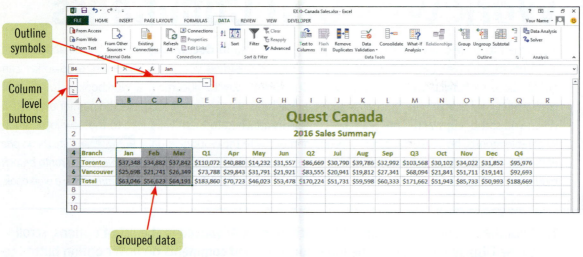

Outline symbols

Column level buttons

Grouped data

FIGURE O-6: Quarter summary

Breaks in column letter sequence indicate data is grouped

Branch	Q1	Q2	Q3	Q4
Toronto	$110,072	$86,669	$103,568	$95,976
Vancouver	$73,788	$83,555	$68,094	$92,693
Total	$183,860	$170,224	$171,662	$188,669

Applying and viewing advanced workbook properties

You can add summary information to your workbook, such as a subject, manager name, company name, or a category, using advanced properties. To view a workbook's advanced properties, click the FILE tab, click Info, click the Properties list arrow on the right side of Backstage view, then click Advanced Properties.

The General tab displays file information. Use the Summary tab to add additional properties to the workbook. The Statistics tab displays file information and the Contents tab lists the file's worksheets. You can create and enter additional information fields on the Custom tab.

Work with Cell Comments

Learning Outcomes
- Insert a new comment
- Show worksheet comments
- Print worksheet comments

If you plan to share a workbook with others, it's a good idea to **document**, or make notes about, basic assumptions, complex formulas, or questionable data. By reading your documentation, a coworker can quickly become familiar with your workbook. The easiest way to document a workbook is to use **cell comments**, which are notes attached to individual cells that appear when you place the pointer over a cell. When you sort or copy and paste cells, any comments attached to them will move to the new location. In PivotTable reports, however, the comments do not move with the worksheet data. **CASE** *Kate thinks one of the figures in the worksheet may be incorrect. She asks you to add a comment for Mark Ng, the Toronto branch manager, pointing out the possible error. You will start by checking the default settings for comments in a workbook.*

STEPS

1. **Click the FILE tab if necessary, click Options, click Advanced in the list of options, scroll to the Display section, click the Indicators only, and comments on hover option button to select it in the "For cells with comments, show:" section if necessary, then click OK**

   The other options in the "For cells with comments, show:" area allow you to display the comment and its indicator or no comments.

QUICK TIP

To copy only comments into a cell, copy the cell contents, right-click the destination cell, point to Paste Special, click Paste Special on the shortcut menu, click Comments in the Paste Special dialog box, then click OK.

2. **Click the Sales sheet tab, click cell F5, click the REVIEW tab, then click the New Comment button in the Comments group**

   The Comment box opens, as shown in **FIGURE O-7**. Excel automatically includes the computer's username at the beginning of the comment. The **username** is the name that appears in the User name text box of the Excel Options dialog box. The white sizing handles on the border of the Comment box let you resize it.

3. **Type Is this figure correct? It looks low to me., then click outside the Comment box**

   A red triangle appears in the upper-right corner of cell F5, indicating that a comment is attached to the cell. People who use your worksheet can easily display comments.

4. **Place the pointer over cell F5**

   The comment appears next to the cell. When you move the pointer outside of cell F5, the comment disappears. Kate asks you to add a comment to cell L6.

5. **Right-click cell L6, click Insert Comment on the shortcut menu, type Is this increase due to the new marketing campaign?, then click outside the Comment box**

   Kate asks you to delete a comment and edit a comment. You start by displaying all worksheet comments.

6. **Click cell A1, then click the Show All Comments button in the Comments group**

   The two worksheet comments are displayed on the screen, as shown in **FIGURE O-8**.

7. **Click the Next button in the Comments group, with the comment in cell F5 selected click the Delete button in the Comments group, click the Next button in the Comments group, click the Edit Comment button in the Comments group, type Mark - at the beginning of the comment in the Comment box, click cell A1, then click the Show All Comments button in the Comments group**

   The Show All Comments button is a toggle button: You click it once to display comments, then click it again to hide comments. You decide to fit the worksheet to print on one page and preview the worksheet and the cell comment along with its associated cell reference on separate pages.

8. **Click the FILE tab, click Print, click Page Setup at the bottom of the Print pane, click the Fit to option button on the Page tab, click the Sheet tab, under Print click the Comments list arrow, click At end of sheet, click OK, then click the Next Page arrow ▶ at the bottom of the preview pane to view the comments**

   Your comment appears on a separate page after the worksheet.

9. **Save the workbook**

Customizing Excel and Advanced Worksheet Management

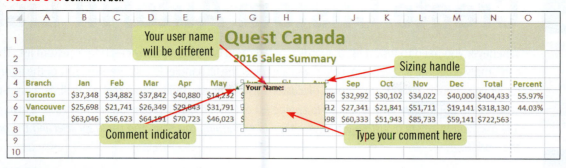

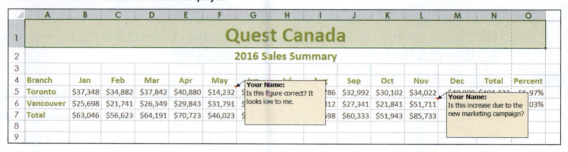

Working with Excel files

To increase your productivity, you can personalize the way recently used files and folders appear in Backstage view. For example, you can keep a workbook displayed in the Recent list of workbooks by clicking the FILE tab, clicking Open, right-clicking the file you want to keep, then clicking Pin to list. You can unpin the file by clicking the pin button to the right of the workbook name. If you want to clear the unpinned workbooks from the Recent list, click the FILE tab, click Open, click Recent Workbooks, right-click a file you want to remove from the list, click Clear unpinned Workbooks, then click Yes.

If you accidently close a file without saving it, if an unstable program causes Excel to close abnormally, or if the power fails,

you can recover your workbook, provided the AutoRecover feature is enabled. To enable AutoRecover, click the FILE tab, click Options, click Save in the Excel Options dialog box, verify that the Save AutoRecover information check box is selected; if necessary, modify the number of minutes AutoRecover saves your files by clicking the up or down arrow to adjust the number of minutes, then click OK. The AutoSave feature automatically saves your work at predetermined intervals, while the AutoRecover feature allows you to recover an AutoSaved file. If you need to restore an AutoRecovered file, click the FILE tab, click Info, click Manage Versions, then click Recover Unsaved Workbooks to see a list of any AutoRecovered files.

Excel 2013

Create Custom AutoFill Lists

Learning Outcomes
• Create a custom list
• Use a custom list

Whenever you need to type a list of words regularly, you can save time by creating a custom list. Then you can simply enter the first value in a blank cell and drag the fill handle. Excel enters the rest of the information for you. **FIGURE O-9** shows examples of custom lists that are built into Excel as well as a user-created custom list. **CASE** ▶ *Kate often has to enter a list of Quest's sales representatives' names in her worksheets. She asks you to create a custom list to save time in performing this task. You begin by selecting the names in the worksheet.*

STEPS

TROUBLE

If a list of sales representatives already appears in the Custom lists box, the person using the computer before you forgot to delete it. Click the list, click Delete, click OK, then proceed with Step 3. It isn't possible to delete the four default lists for days and months.

1. **Click the Jan sheet tab, then select the range A5:A24**

2. **Click the FILE tab, click Options, click Advanced, scroll down to the General section, then click Edit Custom Lists**

   The Custom Lists dialog box displays the custom lists that are already built into Excel, as shown in **FIGURE O-10**. You want to define a custom list containing the sales representatives' names you selected in column A. The Import list from cells text box contains the range you selected in Step 1.

3. **Click Import**

   The list of names is highlighted in the Custom lists box and appears in the List entries box. You decide to test the custom list by placing it in a blank worksheet.

4. **Click OK to confirm the list, click OK again, click the Feb sheet tab, type Garceau in cell A1, then click the Enter button ☑ on the formula bar**

QUICK TIP

You can also drag the fill handle to the right to enter a custom list.

5. **Drag the fill handle to fill the range A2:A20**

   The highlighted range now contains the custom list of sales representatives you created. Kate informs you that sales representative Brady has been replaced by a new representative, Perez. You update the custom list to reflect this change.

6. **Click the FILE tab, click Options, click Advanced, scroll down to the General section, click Edit Custom Lists, click the list of sales representatives names in the Custom lists box, change Brady to Perez in the List entries box, click OK to confirm the change, then click OK again**

   You decide to check the new list to be sure it is accurate.

7. **Click cell C1, type Garceau, click ☑ on the formula bar, drag the fill handle to fill the range C2:C20**

   The highlighted range contains the updated custom list of sales representatives, as shown in **FIGURE O-11**. You've finished creating and editing your custom list, and you need to delete it from the Custom Lists dialog box in case others will be using your computer.

8. **Click the FILE tab, click Options, click Advanced, scroll down to the General section, click Edit Custom Lists, click the list of sales representatives' names in the Custom lists box, click Delete, click OK to confirm the deletion, then click OK two more times**

9. **Save the workbook**

Customizing Excel and Advanced Worksheet Management

FIGURE O-9: Sample custom lists

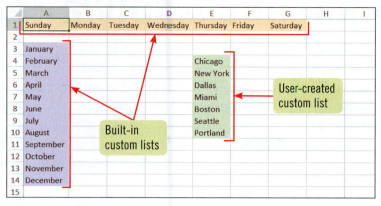

FIGURE O-10: Custom Lists dialog box

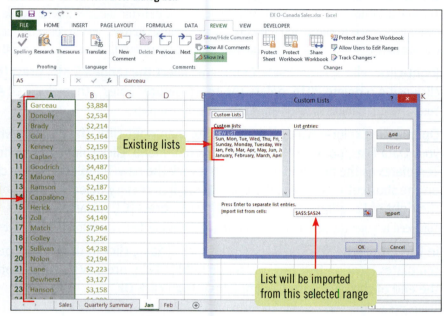

FIGURE O-11: Custom lists with sales rep names

Excel 2013

Create and Apply a Template

Learning Outcomes
• Create a template
• Apply a template

A template is a workbook with an .xltx file extension that contains text, formulas, macros, and formatting that you use repeatedly. Once you save a workbook as a template, it provides a model for creating a new workbook without your having to reenter standard data. To use a template, you **apply** it, which means you create workbooks *based on* the template. A workbook based on a template has the same content, formulas, and formatting you defined in the template, and is saved in the .xlsx format. The template file itself remains unchanged. **CASE** ▶ *Kate plans to use the same formulas, titles, and row and column labels from the Sales worksheet for subsequent yearly worksheets. She asks you to create a template that will allow her to quickly prepare these worksheets.*

STEPS

1. **Delete the Quarterly Summary, Jan, and Feb sheets**

   The workbook now contains only the Sales sheet. You decide to use the Sales sheet structure and formulas as the basis for your new template. You want to leave the formulas in row 7 and in columns N and O so future users will not have to re-create them. But you want to delete the comment, the sales data, and the year 2016.

   TROUBLE
   The divide-by-zero error messages in column O are only temporary and will disappear as soon as Kate opens a document based on the template, saves it as a workbook, and begins to enter next year's data.

2. **Right-click cell L6, click Delete Comment, select the range B5:M6, press [Delete], double-click cell A2, delete 2016, delete the space before "Sales", then click cell A1**

   You will create a folder named Templates to save the template.

3. **Open a File Explorer window, navigate to, then right-click, the location where you store your Data Files, point to New on the shortcut menu, click Folder, enter the name Templates as the new folder name, right click the new Templates folder, click Properties on the shortcut menu, click the General tab if necessary, select the path of the folder to the right of Location:, press and hold [CTRL], press [C], release both keys, then click OK**

   You need to enter the path to your Templates folder as the destination for your saved templates.

4. **In Excel, click the FILE tab, click Options, click Save, click in the Default personal templates location text box, press and hold [CTRL], press [V], release both keys, scroll to the end of the path, enter \Templates\, then click OK**

   Templates will now be saved to the path of your Templates folder. You will save the completed template shown in **FIGURE O-12** so Kate can use it for next year's sales summary.

5. **Click the FILE tab, click Save As, click Browse navigate to the location where you store your Data Files, double-click the Templates folder to open it, click the Save as type list arrow, click Excel Template (*.xltx), then click Save**

   Excel adds the .xltx extension to the filename.

6. **Close the workbook and exit Excel**

   Now you open a workbook based on the Canada Sales template.

   QUICK TIP
   If you want to edit the template, open Excel first and then open the template (the .xltx file). After making changes to the template, save it under the same name in the same location. The changes are applied only to new documents you create that are based on the template.

7. **Navigate to the location where you store your Data Files, double-click the Templates folder to open it, then double-click the EX O-Canada Sales.xltx to open a workbook based on the template**

   The workbook name is EX O-Canada Sales1 as shown in **FIGURE O-13**. A workbook based on a template opens with the template name with a "1" at the end of the name. You want to make sure the formulas are working correctly.

8. **Click cell B5, enter 200, click cell B6, enter 300, select the range B5:B6, copy the data into the range C5:M6, compare your workbook to FIGURE O-14, save the workbook as EX O-Template Test, close the workbook, then submit the workbook to your instructor**

FIGURE O-12: Completed template

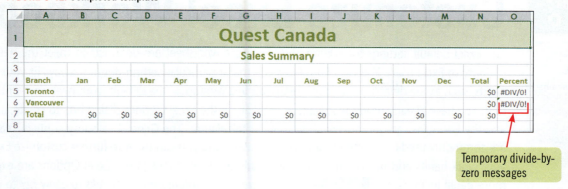

	Branch	Jan	Feb	Mar	Apr	May	Jun	Jul	Aug	Sep	Oct	Nov	Dec	Total	Percent
5	Toronto													$0	#DIV/0!
6	Vancouver													$0	#DIV/0!
7	Total	$0	$0	$0	$0	$0	$0	$0	$0	$0	$0	$0	$0	$0	

Temporary divide-by-zero messages

FIGURE O-13: Workbook based on template

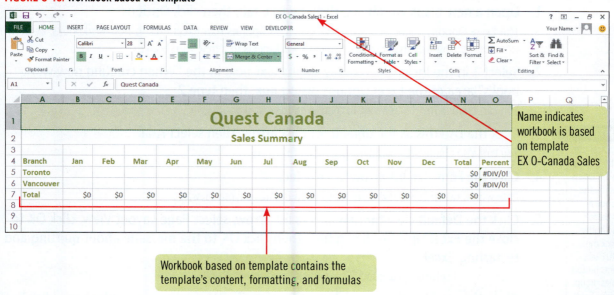

Name indicates workbook is based on template EX O-Canada Sales

Workbook based on template contains the template's content, formatting, and formulas

FIGURE O-14: Completed template test

	Branch	Jan	Feb	Mar	Apr	May	Jun	Jul	Aug	Sep	Oct	Nov	Dec	Total	Percent
5	Toronto	$200	$200	$200	$200	$200	$200	$200	$200	$200	$200	$200	$200	$2,400	40.00%
6	Vancouver	$300	$300	$300	$300	$300	$300	$300	$300	$300	$300	$300	$300	$3,600	60.00%
7	Total	$500	$500	$500	$500	$500	$500	$500	$500	$500	$500	$500	$500	$6,000	

Customize Excel Workbooks

Learning Outcomes
• Change the number of default worksheets
• Change the default workbook font and view

The Excel default settings for editing and viewing a worksheet are designed to meet the needs of the majority of Excel users. You may find, however, that a particular setting doesn't always fit your particular needs, such as the default number of worksheets in a workbook, the default worksheet view, or the default font. You have already used the Advanced category in the Excel Options dialog box to create custom lists and the Formulas category to switch to manual calculation. The General category contains features that are commonly used by a large number of Excel users, and you can use it to further customize Excel to suit your work habits and needs. The most commonly used categories of the Excel Options are explained in more detail in **TABLE O-1**. **CASE** *Kate is interested in customizing workbooks to allow her to work more efficiently. She asks you to use a blank workbook to explore features that will help her better manage her data. In the last workbook you prepared for Kate you had to add a second worksheet. You would like to have two worksheets displayed rather than one when a new workbook is opened.*

STEPS

1. **Open a new blank workbook, click the FILE tab, then click Options**
   The Excel Options dialog box displays the default options that Excel uses in new workbooks, as shown in **FIGURE O-15**. You will change the number of worksheets in a new workbook.

2. **Select 1 in the Include this many sheets text box, in the "When creating new workbooks" area of the Excel Options dialog box, then type 2**
   You can change the default font Excel uses in new workbooks.

3. **Click the Use this as the default font list arrow, then select Arial**
   You can also change the standard workbook font size.

4. **Click the Font size list arrow, then select 12**
   Kate would rather have new workbooks open in Page Layout view.

5. **Click the Default view for new sheets list arrow, select Page Layout View, click OK to close the Excel Options dialog box, then click OK to the message about quitting and restarting Excel**
   These default settings take effect after you exit and restart Excel.

6. **Close the workbook, exit Excel, start Excel again, then open a new blank workbook**
   A new workbook opens with two sheet tabs in Page Layout view and a 12-point Arial font, as shown in **FIGURE O-16**. Now that you have finished exploring the Excel workbook Options, you need to restore the original Excel settings.

7. **Click the FILE tab, click Options, in the "When creating new workbooks" area of the General options, select 2 in the Include this many sheets text box, enter 1, click the Use this as the default font list arrow, select Body Font, select 12 in the Font size text box, type 11, click the Default view for new sheets list arrow, select Normal View, click OK, then close the workbook and exit Excel**

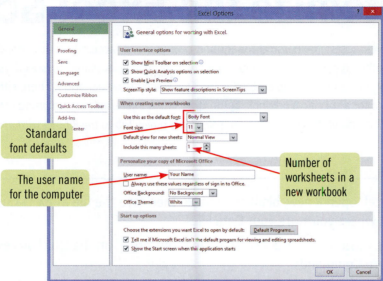

Standard font defaults

The user name for the computer

Number of worksheets in a new workbook

FIGURE O-16: Workbook with new default settings

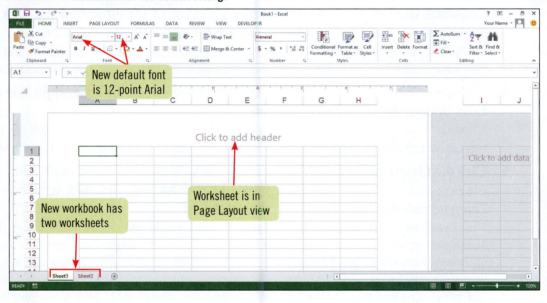

New default font is 12-point Arial

Worksheet is in Page Layout view

New workbook has two worksheets

Excel 2013

TABLE O-1: Categories of Excel options

category	allows you to
General	Change the user name and the workbook screen display
Formulas	Control how the worksheet is calculated, how formulas appear, and error checking settings and rules
Proofing	Control AutoCorrect and spell-checking options
Save	Select a default format and location for saving files, and customize AutoRecover settings
Language	Control the languages displayed and allows you to add languages
Advanced	Create custom lists as well as customize editing and display options
Customize Ribbon	Add tabs and groups to the Ribbon
Quick Access Toolbar	Add commands to the Quick Access toolbar
Add-Ins	Install Excel Add-in programs such as Solver and Analysis ToolPak
Trust Center	Change Trust Center settings to protect your Excel files

Customizing Excel and Advanced Worksheet Management

Customize the Excel Screen

While the Quick Access toolbar and the Ribbon give you easy access to many useful Excel features, you might have other commands that you want to have readily available to speed your work. The Excel Options dialog box allows you to customize the Quick Access toolbar and Ribbon, either for all workbooks (the default) or for a specific workbook. **CASE** ▶ *Kate is interested in customizing the Quick Access toolbar to include spell checking. She would also like you to add a new tab to the Ribbon with accessibility tools.*

STEPS

1. **Start Excel, open a new, blank workbook, then save the file as EX O-Customized in the location where you store your Data Files**

2. **Click the Customize Quick Access Toolbar button ▼ on the Quick Access toolbar, then click More Commands**

   The Excel Options dialog box opens with the Quick Access Toolbar option selected as shown in **FIGURE O-17**. You want to add the spell checking feature to the Quick Access toolbar for the EX O-Customized workbook.

3. **Make sure Popular Commands is displayed in the Choose commands from list, click the Customize Quick Access Toolbar list arrow, select For EX O-Customized.xlsx, click the Spelling command in the Popular Commands list, click Add, then click OK**

   The Spelling button now appears on the Quick Access toolbar to the right of the Save, Undo, and Redo buttons, which appear by default. Kate wants you to add a tab to the Ribbon with a group of accessibility tools.

4. **Click the FILE tab, click Options, click Customize Ribbon, on the lower-right side of the Excel Options dialog box click New Tab**

   A new tab named New Tab (Custom) appears in the listing of Main Tabs below the HOME tab. Under the new tab is a new group named New Group (Custom). You want to add accessibility tools to the new group.

5. **Click the Choose commands from list arrow, click Commands Not in the Ribbon, click the Accessibility Checker command, click Add, click Alt Text, click Add, scroll down, click Zoom In, click Add, click Zoom Out, then click Add**

   Four accessibility tools now appear in the custom group on the new custom tab. Clicking the Check Accessibility button inspects your worksheet for features that need additional description for people with disabilities. Warnings are issued for worksheets with the default names as well as objects such as images and hyperlinks without alternative text. You can also check a worksheet's accessibility features by clicking the FILE tab, clicking Info, clicking the Check for Issues list arrow, then clicking Check Accessibility. You decide to rename the tab and the group to identify the buttons.

6. **Click New Tab (Custom) in the Main Tabs area, click Rename, in the Rename dialog box type ACCESSIBILITY, click OK, click New Group (Custom) below the ACCESSIBILITY tab, click Rename, in the Rename dialog box type Accessibility Tools in the Display name text box, click OK, then click OK again**

   The new custom tab appears in the Ribbon, just to the right of the HOME tab. You can change the order of the tabs using the Move Up ▲ and Move Down ▼ buttons. You decide to check it to verify it contains the buttons you want.

7. **Click the ACCESSIBILITY tab, compare your tab to FIGURE O-18, click the Zoom In button, then click the Zoom Out button**

   You will reset the Ribbon to the default settings.

8. **Click the FILE tab, click Options, click Customize Ribbon, on the lower-right side of the Excel Options dialog box click Reset, click Reset all customizations, click Yes, click OK, save the workbook, then close it and exit Excel**

Customizing Excel and Advanced Worksheet Management

FIGURE O-17: Quick Access Toolbar category of Excel options

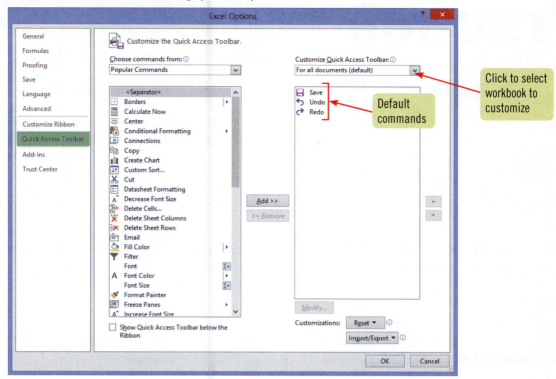

Click to select workbook to customize

Default commands

FIGURE O-18: Workbook with new toolbar button and Accessibility Tab

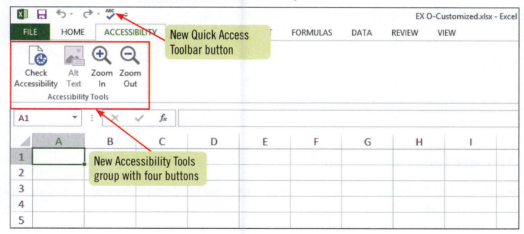

New Quick Access Toolbar button

New Accessibility Tools group with four buttons

Customizing the Quick Access toolbar

You can quickly add a button from the Ribbon to the Quick Access toolbar by right-clicking it and selecting Add to Quick Access Toolbar. Right-clicking a Ribbon button also allows you to quickly customize the Ribbon and the Quick Access toolbar. You can also move the Quick Access toolbar from its default position and minimize the Ribbon.

Practice

Concepts Review

FIGURE O-19

Which element do you click to:

1. Locate cells that reference the active cell?
2. Eliminate tracers from a worksheet?
3. Step through a formula in a selected cell?
4. Locate formula errors in a worksheet?
5. Find cells that may have caused a formula error?

Match each term with the statement that best describes it.

6. [Shift][F9]
7. Outline symbols
8. Custom list
9. Template
10. Comment

a. Note that appears when you place the pointer over a cell
b. Used to hide and display details in grouped data
c. Calculates the worksheet manually
d. A workbook with an .xltx file extension that contains text, formulas, and formatting
e. Entered in a worksheet using the fill handle

Select the best answer from the list of choices.

11. Which of the following categories of Excel options allows you to change the number of default worksheets in a workbook?
    a. General
    b. Proofing
    c. Advanced
    d. Formulas

12. Which of the following categories of Excel options allows you to create Custom Lists?
    a. Add-Ins
    b. Advanced
    c. Customize
    d. Formulas

13. The _____ displays the fewest details in grouped data.
    a. Column Level 2 button
    b. Column Level 1 button
    c. Column Level 3 button
    d. Column Level 4 button

14. To apply a custom list, you:
    a. Click the Fill tab in the Edit dialog box.
    b. Type the first cell entry and drag the fill handle.
    c. Press [Shift][F9].
    d. Select the list in the worksheet.

Customizing Excel and Advanced Worksheet Management

Skills Review

1. **Audit a worksheet.**
   a. Start Excel, open the file EX O-2.xlsx from the location where you store your Data Files, then save it as **EX O-Chatham**.
   b. Select cell B10, then use the Trace Dependents button to locate all the cells that depend on this cell.
   c. Clear the arrows from the worksheet.
   d. Select cell B19, use the Trace Precedents button to find the cells on which that figure is based, then correct the formula in cell B19. (*Hint*: It should be B7–B18.)
   e. Use the Error Checking button to check the worksheet for any other errors. Correct any worksheet errors using the formula bar. (*Hint*: If you get an inconsistent formula error for cell F18, make sure it is totaled vertically or horizontally, then ignore the error.)

2. **Control worksheet calculations.**
   a. Open the Formulas category of the Excel Options dialog box.
   b. Change the worksheet calculations to manual.
   c. Change the figure in cell B6 to **22,000**.
   d. Recalculate the worksheet manually, using an appropriate key combination or button.
   e. Change the worksheet calculations back to automatic using the Calculation Options button, and save the workbook.

3. **Group worksheet data.**
   a. Group the income information in rows 5 and 6.
   b. Group the expenses information in rows 10 through 17.
   c. Hide the income details in rows 5 and 6.
   d. Hide the expenses details in rows 10 through 17.
   e. Enter your name in the center section of the worksheet footer, then preview the worksheet with the income and expenses detail hidden.
   f. Redisplay the income and expenses details.
   g. Remove the row grouping for the income and expenses details. (*Hint*: With the grouped rows selected, click the DATA tab, then click the Ungroup button in the Outline group.)
   h. Save the workbook.

4. **Work with cell comments.**
   a. Insert a comment in cell E12 that reads **Does this include newspaper advertising?**.
   b. Click anywhere outside the Comment box to close it.
   c. Display the comment by moving the pointer over cell E12, then check it for accuracy.
   d. Edit the comment in cell E12 to read **Does this include newspaper and magazine advertising?**.
   e. Preview the worksheet and your comment, with the comment appearing at the end of the sheet.
   f. Save the workbook.

5. **Create custom AutoFill lists.**
   a. Select the range A4:A19.
   b. Open the Custom Lists dialog box, and import the selected text.
   c. Close the dialog box.
   d. Add a worksheet to the workbook. On Sheet2, enter **Income** in cell A1.
   e. Use the fill handle to enter the list through cell A15.
   f. Enter your name in the center section of the Sheet2 footer, then preview the worksheet.
   g. Open the Custom Lists dialog box again, delete the custom list you just created, then save the workbook.

6. **Create and apply a template.**
   a. Delete Sheet2 from the workbook.
   b. Delete the comment in cell E12.
   c. Delete the income and expense data for all four quarters. Leave the worksheet formulas intact.

Skills Review (continued)

   d. Save the workbook as a template with the name **EX O-Chatham.xltx** in the template folder in the location where you store your Data Files. (*Hint*: If you don't have a template folder you will need to create one.)

   e. Close the template, then open a workbook based on the template by opening File Explorer, then double-clicking the template in the template folder in the location where you store your Data Files.

   f. Test the template by entering the data for all four quarters and in every budget category shown in **FIGURE O-20**.

   g. Save the workbook as **EX O-Chatham1.xlsx** in the location where you store your Data Files.

   h. Preview the worksheet, close the workbook, then submit the workbook to your instructor.

7. Customize Excel workbooks.

   a. Open a new workbook, then open the General options of the Excel Options dialog box.

   b. Change the number of sheets in a new workbook to **3**.

   c. Change the default font of a new workbook to 14-point Times New Roman.

   d. Close the workbook and exit Excel.

   e. Start Excel and verify that the new workbook's font is 14-point Times New Roman and that it has three worksheets.

   f. Reset the default number of worksheets to **1** and the default workbook font to 11-point Body Font.

8. Customize the Excel screen.

   a. Use the Quick Access Toolbar category of the Excel Options dialog box to add the Print Preview and Print button to the Quick Access toolbar.

   b. Use the Customize Ribbon category to add a tab named **MATH** to the Ribbon with a group named **Math Tools** containing the buttons Equation and Equation Symbols. (*Hint*: These buttons are in the All Commands list.)

   c. Compare your Quick Access Toolbar and Ribbon to **FIGURE O-21**.

   d. Reset all customizations of the workbook, close the workbook then exit Excel.

FIGURE O-20

	A	B	C	D	E	F	G
1	Chatham Chowder House						
2							
3		Q1	Q2	Q3	Q4	Total	% of Total
4	**Income**						
5	Beverages	$2,000	$2,000	$2,000	$2,000	$8,000	40%
6	Chowder	$3,000	$3,000	$3,000	$3,000	$12,000	60%
7	**Net Sales**	$5,000	$5,000	$5,000	$5,000	$20,000	
8							
9	**Expenses**						
10	Salaries	$100	$100	$100	$100	$400	3%
11	Rent	$200	$200	$200	$200	$800	6%
12	Advertising	$300	$300	$300	$300	$1,200	8%
13	Cleaning	$400	$400	$400	$400	$1,600	11%
14	Fish	$500	$500	$500	$500	$2,000	14%
15	Dairy	$600	$600	$600	$600	$2,400	17%
16	Beverages	$700	$700	$700	$700	$2,800	19%
17	Paper Products	$800	$800	$800	$800	$3,200	22%
18	**Total Expenses**	$3,600	$3,600	$3,600	$3,600	$14,400	100%
19	**Net Profit**	$1,400	$1,400	$1,400	$1,400	$5,600	

FIGURE O-21

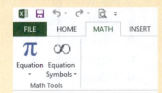

Independent Challenge 1

You are the VP of Human Resources at Connect, a PR firm with offices in the east and the west regions of the United States. You are tracking the overtime hours for workers using total and percentage formulas. Before you begin your analysis, you want to check the worksheet for formula errors. Then, you group the first quarter data, add a comment to the worksheet, and create a custom list of the east and west locations and total labels.

   a. Start Excel, open the file titled EX O-3.xlsx from the location where you store your Data Files, then save it as **EX O-Hours**.

   b. Audit the worksheet, ignoring warnings that aren't errors and correcting the formula errors in the formula bar.

   c. Select cell R5 and use the Trace Precedents button to show the cells used in its formula.

   d. Select cell B10 and use the Trace Dependents button to show the cells affected by the value in the cell.

Independent Challenge 1 (continued)

e. Remove all arrows from the worksheet.

f. Group the months Jan, Feb, and March, then use the Outline symbols to hide the first quarter details.

g. Add the comment **This looks low**. to cell P11. Display the comment on the worksheet so it is visible even when you are not hovering over the cell.

h. Create a custom list by importing the range A5:A15. Add a new worksheet to the workbook, then test the list in cells A1:A11 of the new worksheet. Delete the custom list.

i. Change the comment display to show only the comment indicators and the comments when hovering over the cell with the comment.

j. Add your name to the center section of the worksheet footer, preview the worksheet with the comment on a separate page, then save the workbook.

k. Close the workbook, exit Excel, then submit the workbook to your instructor.

Independent Challenge 2

You are the property manager of The Eastern Group, a commercial retail property located in Baltimore. One of your responsibilities is to keep track of the property's regular monthly expenses. You have compiled a list of fixed expenses in an Excel workbook. Because the expense categories don't change from month to month, you want to create a custom list including each expense item to save time in preparing similar worksheets in the future. You will also temporarily switch to manual formula calculation, check the total formula, and document the data.

a. Start Excel, open the file titled EX O-4.xlsx from the location where you store your Data Files, then save it as **EX O-Expenses**.

b. Select the range of cells A4:A15 on the Fixed Expenses sheet, then import the list to create a Custom List.

c. Add a new worksheet to the workbook, then use the fill handle to insert your list in cells A1:A12 in the new sheet.

d. Add your name to the center section of the new worksheet footer, save the workbook, then preview the worksheet.

e. Delete your custom list, then return to the Fixed Expenses sheet.

f. Switch to manual calculation for formulas. Change the expense for Gas to $9,500.00. Calculate the worksheet formula manually. Turn on automatic calculation again.

g. Add the comment **This may increase**. to cell B4. Display the comment on the worksheet so it is visible even when the mouse pointer is not hovering over the cell.

h. Use the Error Checking dialog box for help in correcting the error in cell B16. Verify that the formula is correctly totaling the expenses in column B.

i. Trace the precedents of cell B16. Compare your worksheet to **FIGURE O-22**.

j. Remove the arrow and the comment display from the worksheet, leaving only the indicator displayed. Do not delete the comment from the worksheet cell.

k. Trace the dependents of cell B4. Remove the arrow from the worksheet.

l. Edit the comment in cell B4 to **This shouldn't change much with rate lock.**, and add the comment **This seems low.** to cell B10.

FIGURE O-22

	A	B	C	D	E
1	**The Eastern Group**				
2	**Fixed Monthly Expenses**				
3	Item	Amount	Your Name:		
4	Gas	$ 9,500.00	This may increase.		
5	Electricity	$ 2,657.00			
6	Water & Sewer	$ 3,011.00			
7	Rubbish Removal	$ 2,159.00			
8	Parking & Garage	$ 923.00			
9	Alarm Service	$ 232.00			
10	Cleaning	$ 277.00			
11	Maintenance	$ 2,140.00			
12	Payroll	$ 5,311.00			
13	Supplies	$ 1,209.00			
14	Landscaping	$ 2,521.00			
15	Legal	$ 2,795.00			
16	Total	$ 32,735.00			
17					

Independent Challenge 2 (continued)

m. Use the Next and Previous buttons in the Comments group of the REVIEW tab to move between comments on the worksheet. Delete the comment in cell B10.

n. Add your name to the center section of the Fixed Expenses worksheet footer, save the workbook, then preview the Fixed Expenses worksheet with the comment appearing at the end of the sheet.

o. Close the workbook, exit Excel, then submit your workbook to your instructor.

Independent Challenge 3

As the business manager of a local historic museum you are responsible for the annual budget. You use Excel to track income and expenses using formulas to total each category and to calculate the net cash flow for the organization. You want to customize your workbooks and settings in Excel so you can work more efficiently. You are also interested in grouping your data and creating a template that you can use to build next year's budget.

a. Start Excel, open the file titled EX O-5.xlsx from the location where you store your Data Files, then save it as **EX O-Budget**.

b. Add an icon to the Quick Access toolbar for the EX O-Budget.xlsx workbook to print preview and print a worksheet.

c. Add a tab to the Ribbon named SHAPES with a group named Shape Tools. Add the buttons Down Arrow, Straight Arrow Connector, Straight Connector, and Zoom from the Commands Not in the Ribbon list to the new group. Compare your Ribbon and Quick Access toolbar to **FIGURE O-23**.

FIGURE O-23

d. Add a new worksheet to the workbook, name the new sheet Shapes. Test the new Shape Tools buttons on the Shapes worksheet by clicking each one and dragging an area to test the shapes. Add your name to the center footer section of the Shapes sheet.

e. Test the Print Preview button on the Quick Access toolbar by previewing the Shapes sheet.

f. On the Budget sheet, group rows 4–6 and 9–14, then use the appropriate row-level button to hide the expense and income details, as shown in **FIGURE O-24**.

FIGURE O-24

	A	B	C	D	E	F
1			Annual Budget			
2	Description	1st Qtr	2nd Qtr	3rd Qtr	4th Qtr	Total
3	Income					
7	Income Total	$695,205	$682,500	$704,320	$783,538	$2,865,563
8	Expenses					
15	Expenses Total	$559,008	$612,592	$545,559	$613,124	$2,330,283
16	Net Cash Flow	$136,197	$69,908	$158,761	$170,414	$535,280
17						

Independent Challenge 3 (continued)

g. Add your name to the center section of the worksheet footer, save the workbook, then use the Print Preview button on the Quick Access toolbar to preview the Budget worksheet. Redisplay all rows, using the Outline symbols, then save the workbook.

h. Delete the Shapes worksheet and all data in the Budget sheet, leaving the formulas and labels.

i. Save the workbook as a template named **EX O-Budget** in the Templates folder in the location where you store your Data Files. Close the template file, and open a workbook based on the template. Save the workbook as **EX O-New Budget**.

j. Test the template by entering data for the four quarters. Save the workbook, then preview the worksheet using the Print Preview button on the Quick Access toolbar.

k. Customize Excel so that your workbooks will open with two worksheets in Page Layout view and use 12-point Trebuchet MS font.

l. Reset the Ribbon, close your workbook, exit Excel, and then open a new workbook to confirm the new default workbook settings. Reset the default Excel workbook to open with one sheet in Normal view and the 11-point Body Font. Close the new workbook.

m. Exit Excel, then submit the EX O-Budget and EX O-New Budget workbooks and the template to your instructor.

Independent Challenge 4: Explore

As the east coast sales manager of a marine supply company, you monitor the sales of the sales representatives in your region. You use Excel to track sales using formulas to total each office. Your assistant has created an Excel workbook tracking the sales of the offices in your region with percentages of total sales. You will check the workbook for errors and add features before sending it back to your assistant for his review.

a. Start Excel, open the file titled EX O-6.xlsx from the location where you store your Data Files, then save it as **EX O-Sales**.

b. Audit the worksheet, ignoring warnings that aren't errors and correcting the formula errors in the formula bar.

c. Select cell S5 on the Sales sheet, then open the Evaluate Formula dialog box.

d. In the Evaluate Formula dialog box, click Evaluate three times to see the process of substituting values for cell addresses in the formula and the results of the formula calculations. Close the Evaluate Formula window.

e. Select cell S6, open the Watch Window. (*Hint*: Click the Watch Window button in the Formula Auditing group on the Formulas tab.)

f. Click Add Watch to add cell S6 to the Watch Window, and observe its value in the window as you change cell G6 to $1000. Close the Watch Window.

g. Add the comment **Please recheck this number.** to cell K7. Copy the comment in cell K7 and paste it in cell P5. (*Hint*: After copying cell K7, use the Paste Special option to copy the comment into cell P5.)

h. Using the Summary tab of advanced workbook properties, add your name as the author, and **Annual Sales** as the Category. Create a custom property of Forward to with a value of John Green. (*Hint*: Click the File tab, click Info, click the Properties list arrow, then click Advanced Properties.)

i. Pin the **EX O-Sales** workbook to the Recent list. Unpin the workbook. Clear all unpinned workbooks from the Recent list.

j. Save the workbook. View any unsaved workbooks.

k. Add your name to the center section of the worksheet footer, save the workbook, then preview the worksheet. Close the workbook, exit Excel, then submit the workbook to your instructor.

Visual Workshop

Open the Data File EX O-7.xlsx from the location where you store your Data Files, then save it as **EX O-Supply**. Group the data as shown after removing any errors in the worksheet. Your grouped results should match **FIGURE O-25**. (*Hint*: The Outline symbols have been hidden for the worksheet.) The new buttons on the Quick Access toolbar have only been added to the EX O-Supply workbook. Add your name to the center section of the worksheet footer, save the workbook, then preview the worksheet. Close the workbook, exit Excel, then submit the workbook to your instructor.

FIGURE O-25

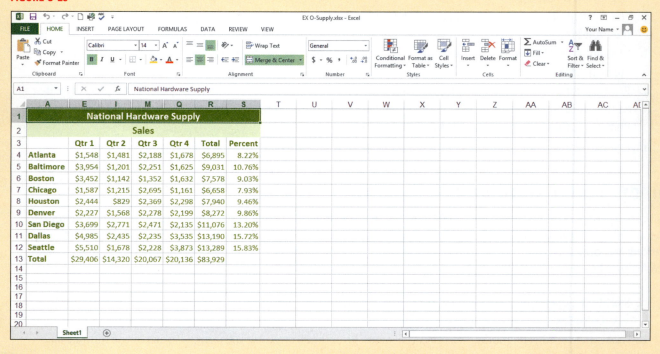

Customizing Excel and Advanced Worksheet Management

Programming
with Excel

CASE ▶ Quest's vice president of sales, Kate Morgan, has used recorded macros to insert worksheet text. Now she would like to automate some more of the division's time-consuming tasks for the sales group. She plans to create macros that she enters manually. You help Kate by creating five new Excel macros using the Visual Basic for Applications (VBA) programming language.

Unit Objectives

After completing this unit, you will be able to:

- View VBA code
- Analyze VBA code
- Write VBA code
- Add a conditional statement

- Prompt the user for data
- Debug a macro
- Create a main procedure
- Run a main procedure

Files You Will Need

EX P-1.xlsm	EX P-5.xlsm
EX P-2.xlsx	EX P-6.xlsm
EX P-3.xlsm	EX P-7.xlsm
EX P-4.xlsm	EX P-8.xlsm

©Katerina Havelkova/Shutterstock

View VBA Code

Learning Outcomes
• Identify the VBA windows
• Define VBA procedure terms

As you learned in Unit I, you can create macros using the Excel macro recorder, which automatically writes Visual Basic for Applications (VBA) instructions for you as you perform actions. For additional flexibility, you can also create entire Excel macros by typing VBA program code. To enter and edit VBA code, you work in the **Visual Basic Editor**, a tool you can start from within Excel. A common method of learning any programming language is to view existing code. In VBA macro code, a sequence of VBA statements is called a **procedure**. The first line of a procedure, called the **procedure header**, defines the procedure's type, name, and arguments. **Arguments** are variables used by other procedures that the main procedure might run. **CASE** ▶ *Each month, Kate receives text files containing tour sales information from the Quest branches. Kate has already imported the text file for the Miami January sales into a worksheet, but she still needs to format it. She asks you to work on a macro to automate the process of formatting the imported information.*

STEPS

TROUBLE
If the DEVELOPER tab does not appear on your Ribbon, click the FILE tab, click Options, click Customize Ribbon on the left side of the Excel Options dialog box, click the Developer check box to select it on the right pane, then click OK.

1. **Start Excel if necessary, open a blank workbook, click the DEVELOPER tab, then click the Macro Security button in the Code group**

   The Trust Center dialog box opens, as shown in **FIGURE P-1**. You know the Quest branch files are from a trusted source, so you decide to allow macros to run in the workbook.

2. **Click the Enable all macros option button if necessary, then click OK**

   You are ready to open a file and view its VBA code. A macro-enabled workbook has the extension .xlsm. Although a workbook containing a macro will open if macros are disabled, they will not function.

3. **Open the file EX P-1.xlsm from the location where you store your Data Files, save it as EX P-Monthly Sales, click the DEVELOPER tab if necessary, then click the Macros button in the Code group**

   The Macro dialog box opens with the FormatFile macro procedure in the list box. If you have any macros saved in your Personal Macro workbook, they are also listed in the Macro dialog box.

4. **If it is not already selected click the FormatFile macro, then click Edit**

   The Microsoft Visual Basic for Applications window opens, containing three windows, shown in **FIGURE P-2**. See **TABLE P-1** to make sure your screen matches the ones shown in this unit. See also the yellow box on the next page for more information about the VBA window.

TROUBLE
To enlarge your Project Explorer window, place the mouse pointer on the right border of the window until it turns into ◀‖▶ then drag the border to the right. Your Project Explorer window may show additional VBA projects.

5. **Make sure both the Visual Basic window and the Code window are maximized to match FIGURE P-2**

   In the Code window, the different parts of the FormatFile procedure appear in various colors. **Comments** are notes explaining the code; they are displayed in green.

6. **Examine the top three lines of code, which contain comments, and the first line of code beginning with Sub FormatFile( )**

   The first two comment lines give the procedure name and tell what the procedure does. The third comment line explains that the keyboard shortcut for this macro procedure is [Ctrl][Shift][F]. Items that appear in blue are **keywords**, which are words Excel recognizes as part of the VBA programming language. The keyword Sub in the procedure header indicates that this is a **Sub procedure**, or a series of Visual Basic statements that perform an action but do not return (create and display) a value. An empty set of parentheses after the procedure name means the procedure doesn't have any arguments. In the next lesson, you will analyze the procedure code to see what each line does.

FIGURE P-1: Macro settings in the Trust Center dialog box

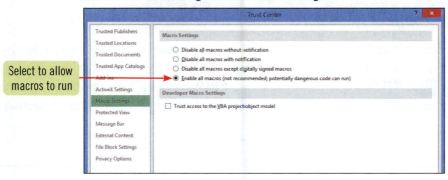

Select to allow macros to run

FIGURE P-2: Procedure displayed in the Visual Basic Editor

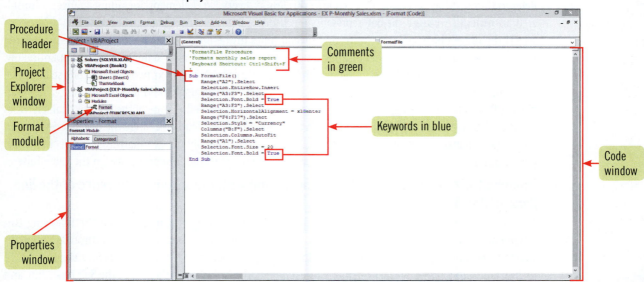

Procedure header

Project Explorer window

Format module

Properties window

Comments in green

Keywords in blue

Code window

TABLE P-1: Matching your screen to the unit figures

if...	do this...
The Properties window is not displayed	Click the Properties Window button on the toolbar
The Project Explorer window is not displayed	Click the Project Explorer button on the toolbar
You see only the Code window	Click Tools on the menu bar, click Options, click the Docking tab, then make sure the Project Explorer and Properties Window options are selected
You do not see folders in the Explorer window	Click the Toggle Folders button on the Project Explorer window Project toolbar

Understanding the Visual Basic Editor

A **module** is the Visual Basic equivalent of a worksheet. In it, you store macro procedures, just as you store data in worksheets. Modules, in turn, are stored in workbooks (or projects), along with worksheets. A **project** is the collection of all procedures in a workbook. You view and edit modules in the Visual Basic Editor, which is made up of the Project Explorer window (also called the Project window), the Code window, and the Properties window. **Project Explorer** displays a list of all open projects (or workbooks) and the worksheets and modules they contain. To view the procedures stored in a module, you must first select the module in Project Explorer (just as you would select a file in Windows Explorer). The **Code window** then displays the selected module's procedures. The **Properties window** displays a list of characteristics (or properties) associated with the module. A newly inserted module has only one property, its name.

Analyze VBA Code

You can learn a lot about the VBA language simply by analyzing the code generated by the Excel macro recorder. The more VBA code you analyze, the easier it is for you to write your own programming code. **CASE** ▶ *Before writing any new procedures, you analyze a previously written procedure that applies formatting to a worksheet. Then you open a worksheet that you want to format and run the macro.*

STEPS

1. **With the FormatFile procedure still displayed in the Code window, examine the next four lines of code, beginning with Range("A2"). Select**

   Refer to **FIGURE P-3** as you analyze the code in this lesson. Every Excel element, including a range, is considered an **object**. A **range object** represents a cell or a range of cells. The statement Range("A2").Select selects the range object cell A2. Notice that several times in the procedure, a line of code (or **statement**) selects a range, and then subsequent lines act on that selection. The next statement, Selection.EntireRow. Insert, inserts a row above the selection, which is currently cell A2. The next two lines of code select range A3:F3 and apply bold formatting to that selection. In VBA terminology, bold formatting is a value of an object's Bold property. A **property** is an attribute of an object that defines one of the object's characteristics (such as size) or an aspect of its behavior (such as whether it is enabled). To change the characteristics of an object, you change the values of its properties. For example, to apply bold formatting to a selected range, you assign the value True to the range's Bold property. To remove bold formatting, assign the value False.

2. **Examine the remaining lines of code, beginning with the second occurrence of the line Range("A3:F3"). Select**

   The next two statements select the range object A3:F3 and center its contents, then the following two statements select the F4:F17 range object and format it as currency. Column objects B through F are then selected, and their widths set to AutoFit. Finally, the range object cell A1 is selected, its font size is changed to 20, and its Bold property is set to True. The last line, End Sub, indicates the end of the Sub procedure and is also referred to as the **procedure footer**.

3. **Click the View Microsoft Excel button 🗙 on the Visual Basic Editor toolbar to return to Excel**

   Because the macro is stored in the EX P-Monthly Sales workbook, Kate can open this workbook and repeatedly use the macro stored there each month after she receives that month's sales data. She wants you to open the workbook containing data for Chicago's January sales and run the macro to format the data. You must leave the EX P-Monthly Sales workbook open to use the macro stored there.

4. **Open the file EX P-2.xlsx from the location where you store your Data Files, then save it as EX P-January Sales**

   This is the workbook containing the data you want to format.

5. **Press [Ctrl][Shift][F] to run the procedure**

   The FormatFile procedure formats the text, as shown in **FIGURE P-4**.

6. **Save the workbook**

   Now that you've successfully viewed and analyzed VBA code and run the macro, you will learn how to write your own code.

FIGURE P-3: VBA code for the FormatFile procedure

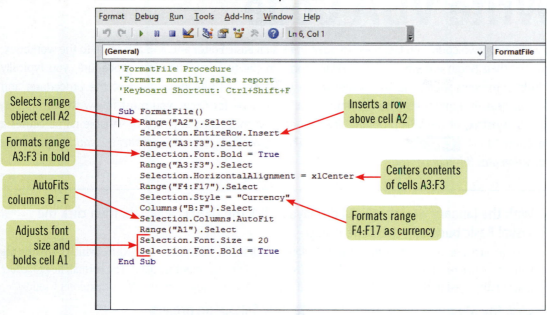

Selects range object cell A2

Formats range A3:F3 in bold

AutoFits columns B - F

Adjusts font size and bolds cell A1

Inserts a row above cell A2

Centers contents of cells A3:F3

Formats range F4:F17 as currency

```
Format   Debug   Run   Tools   Add-Ins   Window   Help
                                              Ln 6, Col 1

(General)                                              FormatFile

    'FormatFile Procedure
    'Formats monthly sales report
    'Keyboard Shortcut: Ctrl+Shift+F
    '
    Sub FormatFile()
        Range("A2").Select
        Selection.EntireRow.Insert
        Range("A3:F3").Select
        Selection.Font.Bold = True
        Range("A3:F3").Select
        Selection.HorizontalAlignment = xlCenter
        Range("F4:F17").Select
        Selection.Style = "Currency"
        Columns("B:F").Select
        Selection.Columns.AutoFit
        Range("A1").Select
        Selection.Font.Size = 20
        Selection.Font.Bold = True
    End Sub
```

FIGURE P-4: Worksheet formatted using the FormatFile procedure

Formatted title

Row inserted

Formatted column headings

Range formatted as currency

	A	B	C	D	E	F	G
1	Quest Chicago January Sales						
2							
3	Trip Code	Depart Date	Number of Days	Seats Sold	Tour	Sales	
4	457R	1/7/2016	30	30	African National Parks	$ 121,400.00	
5	556J	1/13/2016	14	25	Amazing Amazon	$ 67,875.00	
6	675Y	1/19/2016	14	32	Catalonia Adventure	$ 100,300.00	
7	446R	1/20/2016	7	18	Yellowstone	$ 46,958.00	
8	251D	1/21/2016	7	10	Costa Rica	$ 28,220.00	
9	335P	1/22/2016	21	33	Corfu Sailing Voyage	$ 105,270.00	
10	431V	1/25/2016	7	21	Costa Rica Rainforests	$ 54,390.00	
11	215C	1/26/2016	14	19	Silk Road Travels	$ 92,663.00	
12	325B	1/27/2016	10	17	Down Under Exodus	$ 47,600.00	
13	311A	1/29/2016	18	20	Essential India	$ 102,887.00	
14	422R	1/29/2016	7	24	Exotic Morocco	$ 45,600.00	
15	331E	1/30/2016	12	21	Experience Cambodia	$ 98,557.00	
16	831P	1/30/2016	14	15	Galapagos Adventure	$ 55,698.00	
17	337Q	1/31/2016	18	10	Green Adventures in Ecuador	$ 39,574.00	

Columns widened

Write VBA Code

Learning Outcomes
• Create a VBA module
• Enter VBA code

To write your own code, you first need to open the Visual Basic Editor and add a module to the workbook. You can then begin entering the procedure code. In the first few lines of a procedure, you typically include comments indicating the name of the procedure, a brief description of the procedure, and shortcut keys, if applicable. When writing Visual Basic code for Excel, you must follow the formatting rules, or **syntax**, of the VBA programming language. A misspelled keyword or variable name causes a procedure to fail. **CASE** *Kate would like to total the monthly sales. You help her by writing a procedure that automates this routine task.*

STEPS

TROUBLE
If the Code window is empty, verify that the workbook that contains your procedures (EX P-Monthly Sales) is open.

1. **With the January worksheet still displayed, click the DEVELOPER tab, then click the Visual Basic button in the Code group**

   Two projects are displayed in the Project Explorer window, EX P-Monthly Sales.xlsm (which contains the FormatFile macro) and EX P-January Sales.xlsx (which contains the monthly data). The FormatFile procedure is again displayed in the Visual Basic Editor. You may have other projects in the Project Explorer window.

2. **Click the Modules folder in the EX P-Monthly Sales.xlsm project**

   You need to store all of the procedures in the EX P-Monthly Sales.xlsm project, which is in the EX P-Monthly Sales.xlsm workbook. By clicking the Modules folder, you have activated the workbook, and the title bar changes from EX P-January Sales to EX P-Monthly Sales.

3. **Click Insert on the Visual Basic Editor menu bar, then click Module**

   A new, blank module with the default name Module1 appears in the EX P-Monthly Sales.xlsm project, under the Format module. You think the property name of the module could be more descriptive.

4. **Click (Name) in the Properties window, then type Total**

   The module name is Total. The module name should not be the same as the procedure name (which will be AddTotal). In the code shown in FIGURE P-5, comments begin with an apostrophe, and the lines of code under Sub AddTotal( ) have been indented using the Tab key. When you enter the code in the next step, after you type the procedure header Sub AddTotal( ) and press [Enter], the Visual Basic Editor automatically enters End Sub (the procedure footer) in the Code window.

TROUBLE
As you type, you may see words in drop-down lists. This optional feature is explained in the Clues to Use titled "Entering code using AutoComplete" on the next page. For now, just continue to type.

5. **Click in the Code window, then type the procedure code exactly as shown in FIGURE P-5, entering your name in the second line, pressing [Tab] to indent text and [Shift][Tab] to move the insertion point to the left**

   The lines that begin with ActiveCell.Formula insert the information enclosed in quotation marks into the active cell. For example, ActiveCell.Formula = "Monthly Total:" inserts the words "Monthly Total:" into cell E18, the active cell. As you type each line, Excel adjusts the spacing.

6. **Compare the procedure code you entered in the Code window with FIGURE P-5, make any corrections if necessary, then click the Save EX P-Monthly Sales.xlsm button 💾 on the Visual Basic Editor toolbar**

7. **Click the View Microsoft Excel button 🗷 on the toolbar, click EX P-January Sales.xlsx on the taskbar to activate the workbook if necessary, with the January worksheet displayed click the DEVELOPER tab, then click the Macros button in the Code group**

   Macro names have two parts. The first part ('EX P-Monthly Sales.xlsm'!) indicates the workbook where the macro is stored. The second part (AddTotal or FormatFile) is the name of the procedure, taken from the procedure header.

TROUBLE
If an error message appears, click Debug. Click the Reset button 🔳 on the toolbar, correct the error, then repeat Steps 6–8.

8. **Click 'EX P-MonthlySales.xlsm'!AddTotal to select it if necessary, then click Run**

   The AddTotal procedure inserts and formats the monthly total in cell F18, as shown in FIGURE P-6.

9. **Save the workbook**

FIGURE P-5: VBA code for the AddTotal procedure

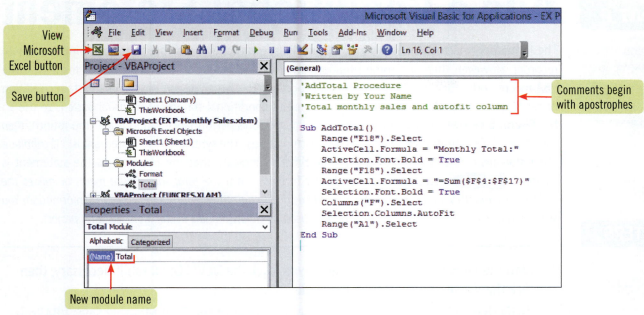

View Microsoft Excel button

Save button

Comments begin with apostrophes

New module name

```vba
'AddTotal Procedure
'Written by Your Name
'Total monthly sales and autofit column
'
Sub AddTotal()
    Range("E18").Select
    ActiveCell.Formula = "Monthly Total:"
    Selection.Font.Bold = True
    Range("F18").Select
    ActiveCell.Formula = "=Sum($F$4:$F$17)"
    Selection.Font.Bold = True
    Columns("F").Select
    Selection.Columns.AutoFit
    Range("A1").Select
End Sub
```

FIGURE P-6: Worksheet after running the AddTotal procedure

	A	B	C	D	E	F	G
1	Quest Chicago January Sales						
2							
3	Trip Code	Depart Date	Number of Days	Seats Sold	Tour	Sales	
4	457R	1/7/2016	30	30	African National Parks	$ 121,400.00	
5	556J	1/13/2016	14	25	Amazing Amazon	$ 67,875.00	
6	675Y	1/19/2016	14	32	Catalonia Adventure	$ 100,300.00	
7	446R	1/20/2016	7	18	Yellowstone	$ 46,958.00	
8	251D	1/21/2016	7	10	Costa Rica	$ 28,220.00	
9	335P	1/22/2016	21	33	Corfu Sailing Voyage	$ 105,270.00	
10	431V	1/25/2016	7	21	Costa Rica Rainforests	$ 54,390.00	
11	215C	1/26/2016	14	19	Silk Road Travels	$ 92,663.00	
12	325B	1/27/2016	10	17	Down Under Exodus	$ 47,600.00	
13	311A	1/29/2016	18	20	Essential India	$ 102,887.00	
14	422R	1/29/2016	7	24	Exotic Morocco	$ 45,600.00	
15	331E	1/30/2016	12	21	Experience Cambodia	$ 98,557.00	
16	831P	1/30/2016	14	15	Galapagos Adventure	$ 55,698.00	
17	337Q	1/31/2016	18	10	Green Adventures in Ecuador	$ 39,574.00	
18					**Monthly Total:**	**$ 1,006,992.00**	

Result of AddTotal procedure

Entering code using AutoComplete

To assist you in entering the VBA code, the Editor uses **AutoComplete**, a list of words that can be used in the macro statement and match what you type. The list usually appears after you press [.] (period). To include a word from the list in the macro statement, select the word in the list, then double-click it or press [Tab]. For example, to enter the Range("E12").Select instruction, type Range("E12"), then press [.] (period). Type s to bring up the words beginning with the letter "s", select the Select command in the list, then press [Tab] to enter the word "Select" in the macro statement.

Add a Conditional Statement

The formatting macros you entered in the previous lesson could have been created using the macro recorder. However, there are some situations where you cannot use the recorder and must type the VBA macro code, such as when you want a procedure to take an action based on a certain condition or set of conditions. One way of adding this type of conditional statement in Visual Basic is to use an **If...Then...Else statement**. For example, *if* a salesperson's performance rating is a 5 (top rating), *then* calculate a 10% bonus; otherwise (*else*), there is no bonus. The syntax for this statement is: "If *condition* Then *statements* Else [*else statements*]." The brackets indicate that the Else part of the statement is optional. **CASE** ▶ *Kate wants the worksheet to point out if the total sales figure meets or misses the $1,000,000 monthly quota. You use Excel to add a conditional statement that indicates this information. You start by returning to the Visual Basic Editor and inserting a new module in the Monthly Sales project.*

STEPS

1. **With the January worksheet still displayed, click the DEVELOPER tab if necessary, then click the Visual Basic button in the Code group**

2. **Verify that the Total module in the Modules folder of the EX P-Monthly Sales VBAProject is selected in the Project Explorer window, click Insert on the Visual Basic Editor menu bar, then click Module**

   A new, blank module named Module1 is inserted in the EX P-Monthly Sales workbook.

3. **In the Properties window click (Name), then type Sales**

4. **Click in the Code window, then type the code exactly as shown in FIGURE P-7, entering your name in the second line**

   Notice the green comment lines in the middle of the code. These lines help explain the procedure.

5. **Compare the procedure you entered with FIGURE P-7, make any corrections if necessary, click the Save EX P-Monthly Sales.xlsm button 🔲 on the Visual Basic Editor toolbar, then click the View Microsoft Excel button 🔲 on the toolbar**

6. **If necessary, click EX P-January Sales.xlsx in the taskbar to display it, click the Macros button in the Code group, in the Macro dialog box click 'EX P-Monthly Sales.xlsm'!SalesStatus, then click Run**

   The SalesStatus procedure indicates the status "Met Quota", as shown in FIGURE P-8.

7. **Save the workbook**

FIGURE P-7: VBA code for the SalesStatus procedure

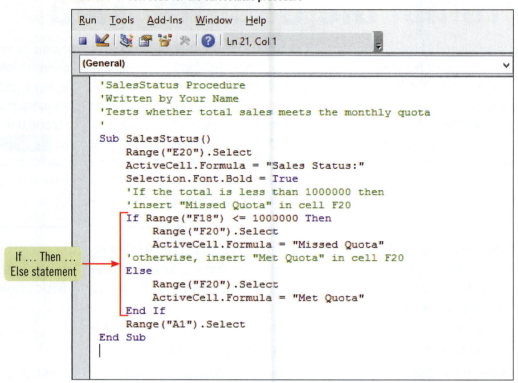

```
Run   Tools   Add-Ins   Window   Help
Ln 21, Col 1

(General)

    'SalesStatus Procedure
    'Written by Your Name
    'Tests whether total sales meets the monthly quota
    '
    Sub SalesStatus()
        Range("E20").Select
        ActiveCell.Formula = "Sales Status:"
        Selection.Font.Bold = True
        'If the total is less than 1000000 then
        'insert "Missed Quota" in cell F20
        If Range("F18") <= 1000000 Then
            Range("F20").Select
            ActiveCell.Formula = "Missed Quota"
        'otherwise, insert "Met Quota" in cell F20
        Else
            Range("F20").Select
            ActiveCell.Formula = "Met Quota"
        End If
        Range("A1").Select
    End Sub
```

If ... Then ... Else statement

FIGURE P-8: Result of running the SalesStatus procedure

1	Quest Chicago January Sales					
2						
3	**Trip Code**	**Depart Date**	**Number of Days**	**Seats Sold**	**Tour**	**Sales**
4	457R	1/7/2016	30	30	African National Parks	$ 121,400.00
5	556J	1/13/2016	14	25	Amazing Amazon	$ 67,875.00
6	675Y	1/19/2016	14	32	Catalonia Adventure	$ 100,300.00
7	446R	1/20/2016	7	18	Yellowstone	$ 46,958.00
8	251D	1/21/2016	7	10	Costa Rica	$ 28,220.00
9	335P	1/22/2016	21	33	Corfu Sailing Voyage	$ 105,270.00
10	431V	1/25/2016	7	21	Costa Rica Rainforests	$ 54,390.00
11	215C	1/26/2016	14	19	Silk Road Travels	$ 92,663.00
12	325B	1/27/2016	10	17	Down Under Exodus	$ 47,600.00
13	311A	1/29/2016	18	20	Essential India	$ 102,887.00
14	422R	1/29/2016	7	24	Exotic Morocco	$ 45,600.00
15	331E	1/30/2016	12	21	Experience Cambodia	$ 98,557.00
16	831P	1/30/2016	14	15	Galapagos Adventure	$ 55,698.00
17	337Q	1/31/2016	18	10	Green Adventures in Ecuador	$ 39,574.00
18					**Monthly Total:**	**$ 1,006,992.00**
19						
20					**Sales Status:**	Met Quota
21						
22						

Indicates status of monthly total

Prompt the User for Data

Another situation where you must type, not record, VBA code is when you need to pause a macro to allow user input. You use the VBA InputBox function to display a dialog box that prompts the user for information. A **function** is a predefined procedure that returns (creates and displays) a value; in this case the value returned is the information the user enters. The required elements of an InputBox function are as follows: *object*.InputBox("*prompt*"), where "*prompt*" is the message that appears in the dialog box. For a detailed description of the InputBox function, use the Visual Basic Editor's Help menu. **CASE** *You decide to create a procedure that will insert the user's name in the left footer area of the worksheet. You use the InputBox function to display a dialog box in which the user can enter his or her name. You also type an intentional error into the procedure code, which you will correct in the next lesson.*

STEPS

1. **With the January worksheet displayed, click the DEVELOPER tab if necessary, click the Visual Basic button in the Code group, verify that the Sales module is selected in the EX P-Monthly Sales VBAProject Modules folder, click Insert on the Visual Basic Editor menu bar, then click Module**

   A new, blank module named Module1 is inserted in the EX P-Monthly Sales workbook.

2. **In the Properties window click (Name), then type Footer**

3. **Click in the Code window, then type the procedure code exactly as shown in FIGURE P-9 entering your name in the second line**

   Like the SalesStatus procedure, this procedure also contains comments that explain the code. The first part of the code, Dim LeftFooterText As String, **declares**, or defines, LeftFooterText as a text string variable. In Visual Basic, a **variable** is a location in memory in which you can temporarily store one item of information. Dim statements are used to declare variables and must be entered in the following format: Dim *variablename* As *datatype*. The datatype here is "string." In this case, you plan to store the information received from the input box in the temporary memory location called LeftFooterText. Then you can place this text in the left footer area. The remaining statements in the procedure are explained in the comment line directly above each statement. Notice the comment pointing out the error in the procedure code. You will correct this in the next lesson.

4. **Review your code, make any necessary changes, click the Save EX P-MonthlySales.xlsm button 🖫 on the Visual Basic Editor toolbar, then click the View Microsoft Excel button ⊠ on the toolbar**

5. **With the January worksheet displayed, click the Macros button in the Code group, in the Macro dialog box click 'EX P-Monthly Sales.xlsm'!FooterInput, then click Run**

   The procedure begins, and a dialog box generated by the InputBox function opens, prompting you to enter your name, as shown in FIGURE P-10.

TROUBLE
If your macro doesn't prompt you for your name, it may contain an error. Return to the Visual Basic Editor, click the Reset button ▣ correct the error by referring to **FIGURE P-9**, then repeat Steps 4 and 5. You'll learn more about how to correct such macro errors in the next lesson.

6. **With the cursor in the text box, type your name, then click OK**

7. **Click the File tab, click Print, then view the worksheet preview**

   Although the customized footer with the date is inserted on the sheet, because of the error your name does *not* appear in the left section of the footer. In the next lesson, you will learn how to step through a procedure's code line by line. This will help you locate the error in the FooterInput procedure.

8. **Click the Back button ⊜, then save the workbook**

   You return to the January worksheet.

FIGURE P-9: VBA code for the FooterInput procedure

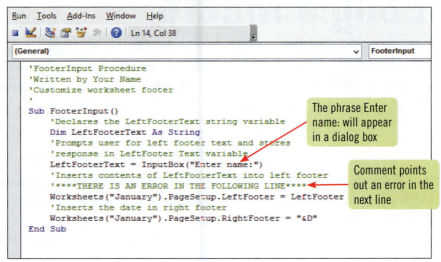

```
Run  Tools  Add-Ins  Window  Help

■ ☒ ☒ ☞ ☞ ⁂ ❘ ❷ ❘ Ln 14, Col 38

(General)                                                    ⌄    FooterInput

    'FooterInput Procedure
    'Written by Your Name
    'Customize worksheet footer
    '
    Sub FooterInput()
        'Declares the LeftFooterText string variable
        Dim LeftFooterText As String
        'Prompts user for left footer text and stores
        'response in LeftFooter Text variable
        LeftFooterText = InputBox("Enter name:")
        'Inserts contents of LeftFooterText into left footer
        '****THERE IS AN ERROR IN THE FOLLOWING LINE****
        Worksheets("January").PageSetup.LeftFooter = LeftFooter
        'Inserts the date in right footer
        Worksheets("January").PageSetup.RightFooter = "&D"
    End Sub
```

The phrase Enter name: will appear in a dialog box

Comment points out an error in the next line

FIGURE P-10: InputBox function's dialog box

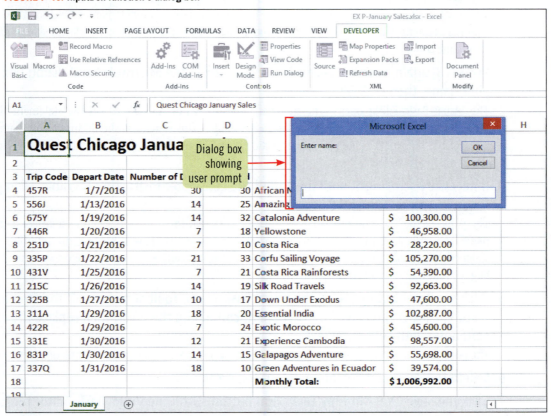

Dialog box showing user prompt

	A	B	C	D		F
1	Quest Chicago Janua					
2						
3	Trip Code	Depart Date	Number of D			
4	457R	1/7/2016	30	30 African N		
5	556J	1/13/2016	14	25 Amazing		
6	675Y	1/19/2016	14	32 Catalonia Adventure	$ 100,300.00	
7	446R	1/20/2016	7	18 Yellowstone	$ 46,958.00	
8	251D	1/21/2016	7	10 Costa Rica	$ 28,220.00	
9	335P	1/22/2016	21	33 Corfu Sailing Voyage	$ 105,270.00	
10	431V	1/25/2016	7	21 Costa Rica Rainforests	$ 54,390.00	
11	215C	1/26/2016	14	19 Silk Road Travels	$ 92,663.00	
12	325B	1/27/2016	10	17 Down Under Exodus	$ 47,600.00	
13	311A	1/29/2016	18	20 Essential India	$ 102,887.00	
14	422R	1/29/2016	7	24 Exotic Morocco	$ 45,600.00	
15	331E	1/30/2016	12	21 Experience Cambodia	$ 98,557.00	
16	831P	1/30/2016	14	15 Galapagos Adventure	$ 55,698.00	
17	337Q	1/31/2016	18	10 Green Adventures in Ecuador	$ 39,574.00	
18				**Monthly Total:**	**$ 1,006,992.00**	

Microsoft Excel — Enter name: — OK — Cancel

Naming variables

Variable names in VBA must begin with a letter. Letters can be uppercase or lowercase. Variable names cannot include periods or spaces, and they can be up to 255 characters long. Each variable name in a procedure must be unique. Examples of valid and invalid variable names are shown in **TABLE P-2**.

TABLE P-2: Variable names

valid	invalid
Sales_Department	Sales Department
SalesDepartment	Sales Department
Quarter1	1stQuarter

© 2014 Cengage Learning

Debug a Macro

When a macro procedure does not run properly, it can be due to an error, referred to as a **bug**, in the code. To help you find the bug(s) in a procedure, the Visual Basic Editor lets you step through the procedure's code, one line at a time. When you locate the error, you can then correct, or **debug**, it. **CASE** *You decide to debug the macro procedure to find out why it failed to insert your name in the worksheet footer.*

STEPS

1. **With the January worksheet displayed, click the DEVELOPER tab if necessary, click the Macros button in the Code group, in the Macro dialog box click 'EX P-Monthly Sales. xlsm'!FooterInput, then click Step Into**

   The Visual Basic Editor opens with the yellow statement selector positioned on the first statement of the procedure, as shown in **FIGURE P-11**.

2. **Press [F8] to step to the next statement**

   The statement selector skips over the comments and the line of code beginning with Dim. The Dim statement indicates that the procedure will store your name in a variable named LeftFooterText. Because Dim is a declaration of a variable and not a procedure statement, the statement selector skips it and moves to the line containing the InputBox function.

3. **Press [F8] again, with the cursor in the text box in the Microsoft Excel dialog box type your name, then click OK**

   The Visual Basic Editor opens. The statement selector is now positioned on the statement that reads Worksheets("January").PageSetup.LeftFooter = LeftFooter. This statement should insert your name (which you just typed in the text box) in the left section of the footer. This is the instruction that does not appear to be working correctly.

4. **If necessary scroll right until the end of the LeftFooter instruction is visible, then place the mouse pointer on LeftFooter**

   The value of the LeftFooter variable is displayed as shown in **FIGURE P-12**. Rather than containing your name, the variable LeftFooter at the end of this line is empty. This is because the InputBox function assigned your name to the LeftFooterText variable, not to the LeftFooter variable. Before you can correct this bug, you need to turn off the Step Into feature.

5. **Click the Reset button 🔲 on the Visual Basic Editor toolbar to turn off the Step Into feature, click at the end of the statement containing the error, then replace the variable LeftFooter with LeftFooterText**

   The revised statement now reads Worksheets("January").PageSetup.LeftFooter = LeftFooterText.

6. **Delete the comment line pointing out the error**

7. **Click the Save EX P-Monthly Sales.xlsm button 🔲 on the Visual Basic Editor toolbar, then click the View Microsoft Excel button 🔲 on the toolbar**

8. **With the January worksheet displayed click the Macros button in the Code group, in the Macro dialog box click 'EX P-Monthly Sales.xlsm'!FooterInput, click Run to rerun the procedure, when prompted type your name, then click OK**

9. **Click the File tab, click Print, then view the worksheet preview**

   Your name now appears in the left section of the footer.

10. **Click the Back button 🔙, then save the workbook**

FIGURE P-11: Statement selector positioned on first procedure statement

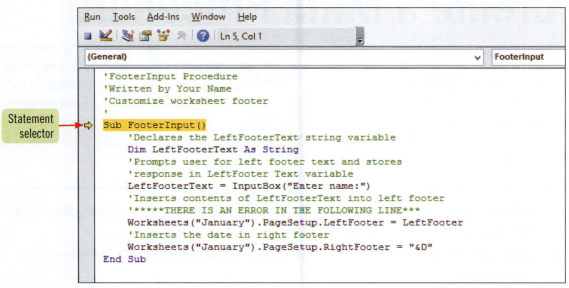

Statement selector →

```
'FooterInput Procedure
'Written by Your Name
'Customize worksheet footer
'
Sub FooterInput()
    'Declares the LeftFooterText string variable
    Dim LeftFooterText As String
    'Prompts user for left footer text and stores
    'response in LeftFooter Text variable
    LeftFooterText = InputBox("Enter name:")
    'Inserts contents of LeftFooterText into left footer
    '*****THERE IS AN ERROR IN THE FOLLOWING LINE***
    Worksheets("January").PageSetup.LeftFooter = LeftFooter
    'Inserts the date in right footer
    Worksheets("January").PageSetup.RightFooter = "&D"
End Sub
```

FIGURE P-12: Value contained in LeftFooter variable

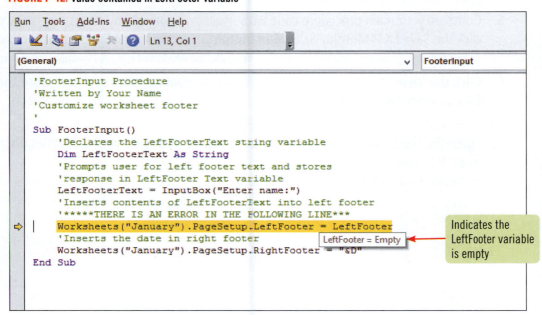

```
'FooterInput Procedure
'Written by Your Name
'Customize worksheet footer
'
Sub FooterInput()
    'Declares the LeftFooterText string variable
    Dim LeftFooterText As String
    'Prompts user for left footer text and stores
    'response in LeftFooter Text variable
    LeftFooterText = InputBox("Enter name:")
    'Inserts contents of LeftFooterText into left footer
    '*****THERE IS AN ERROR IN THE FOLLOWING LINE***
    Worksheets("January").PageSetup.LeftFooter = LeftFooter
    'Inserts the date in right footer
    Worksheets("January").PageSetup.RightFooter = "&D"
End Sub
```

LeftFooter = Empty ← Indicates the LeftFooter variable is empty

Adding security to your macro projects

To add security to your projects, you can add a digital signature to the project. A digital signature guarantees the project hasn't been altered since it was signed. Sign macros only after you have tested them and are ready to distribute them. If the code in a digitally signed macro project is changed in any way, its digital signature is removed. To add a digital signature to a Visual Basic project, select the project that you want to sign in the Visual Basic Project Explorer window, click the Tools menu in the Visual Basic Editor, click Digital Signature, click Choose, select the certificate, then click OK twice. When you add a digital signature to a project, the macro project is automatically re-signed whenever it is saved on your computer. You can get a digital certificate from your administrator. There are also third-party certification authorities that issue certificates that are trusted by Microsoft.

Excel 2013

Create a Main Procedure

Learning Outcome
• Enter a VBA main procedure

When you routinely need to run several macros one after another, you can save time by combining them into one procedure. The resulting procedure, which processes (or runs) multiple procedures in sequence, is referred to as the **main procedure**. To create a main procedure, you type a **Call statement** for each procedure you want to run. The syntax of the Call statement is Call *procedurename*, where *procedurename* is the name of the procedure you want to run. **CASE** *To avoid having to run her macros one after another every month, Kate asks you to create a main procedure that will run (or call) each of the procedures in the EX P-Monthly Sales workbook in sequence.*

STEPS

1. **With the January worksheet displayed, click the DEVELOPER tab if necessary, then click the Visual Basic button in the Code group**

2. **Verify that EX P-Monthly Sales is the active project, click Insert on the menu bar, then click Module**

   A new, blank module named Module1 is inserted in the EX P-Monthly Sales workbook.

3. **In the Properties window click (Name), then type MainProc**

4. **In the Code window enter the procedure code exactly as shown in FIGURE P-13, entering your name in the second line**

5. **Compare your main procedure code with FIGURE P-13, correct any errors if necessary, then click the Save EX P-Monthly Sales.xlsm button 🔲 on the Visual Basic Editor toolbar**

   To test the new main procedure, you need an unformatted version of the EX P-January Sales worksheet.

6. **Click the View Microsoft Excel button 🔳 on the toolbar, then save and close the EX P-January Sales workbook**

   The EX P-Monthly Sales workbook remains open.

7. **Open the file EX P-2.xlsx from the location where you store your Data Files, then save it as EX P-January Sales 2**

   In the next lesson, you'll run the main procedure.

Copying a macro to another workbook

If you would like to use a macro in another workbook, you can copy the module to that workbook using the Visual Basic Editor. Open both the source and destination Excel workbooks, then open the Visual Basic Editor and verify that macros are enabled. In Project Explorer, drag the module that will be copied from the source workbook to the destination workbook.

FIGURE P-13: VBA code for the MainProcedure procedure

```
'MainProcedure Procedure
'Written by Your Name
'Calls sub procedures in sequence
'
Sub MainProcedure()
    Call FormatFile
    Call AddTotal
    Call SalesStatus
    Call FooterInput
End Sub
```

MainProcedure calls each procedure in the order shown

Writing and documenting VBA code

When you write VBA code in the Visual Basic Editor, you want to make it as readable as possible. This makes it easier for you or your coworkers to edit the code when changes need to be made. The procedure statements should be indented, leaving the procedure name and its End statement easy to spot in the code. This is helpful when a module contains many procedures. It is also good practice to add comments at the beginning of each procedure that describe its purpose and any assumptions made in the procedure, such as the quota amounts. You should also explain each code statement with a comment. You have seen comments inserted into VBA code by beginning the statement with an apostrophe. You can also add comments to the end of a line of VBA code by placing an apostrophe before the comment, as shown in **FIGURE P-14**.

FIGURE P-14: VBA code with comments at the end of statements

Run Tools Add-Ins Window Help

Ln 10, Col 8

(General) | MainProcedure

```
'MainProcedure Procedure
'Written by Your Name
'Calls sub procedures in sequence
'
Sub MainProcedure()
    Call FormatFile 'Run FormatFile procedure
    Call AddTotal  'Run AddTotal procedure
    Call SalesStatus  'Run SalesStatus procedure
    Call FooterInput  'Run FooterInput procedure
End Sub
```

Comments at the end of the statements in green

Excel 2013

Run a Main Procedure

Running a main procedure allows you to run several macros in sequence. You can run a main procedure just as you would any other macro procedure. **CASE** ▶ *You have finished creating Kate's main procedure, and you are ready to run it. If the main procedure works correctly, it should format the worksheet, insert the sales total, insert a sales status message, and add your name and date to the worksheet footer.*

STEPS

1. **With the January worksheet displayed, click the DEVELOPER tab, click the Macros button in the Code group, in the Macro dialog box click 'EX P-Monthly Sales.xlsm'!MainProcedure, click Run, when prompted type your name, then click OK**

   The MainProcedure runs the FormatFile, AddTotal, SalesStatus, and FooterInput procedures in sequence. You can see the results of the FormatFile, AddTotal, and SalesStatus procedures in the worksheet window, as shown in **FIGURE P-16**. To view the results of the FooterInput procedure, you need to switch to the Preview window.

2. **Click the File tab, click Print, view the worksheet preview and verify that your name appears in the left footer area and the date appears in the right footer area, click the Back button ⬅, then click the DEVELOPER tab**

3. **Click the Visual Basic button in the Code group**

   You need to add your name to the Format module.

4. **In the Project Explorer window, double-click the Format module, add a comment line after the procedure name that reads Written by [Your Name], then click the Save EX P-Monthly Sales.xlsm button 💾**

   You want to see the options for printing VBA code.

5. **Click File on the Visual Basic Editor menu bar, then click Print**

   The Print - VBAProject dialog box opens, as shown in **FIGURE P-17**. The Current Module is selected which will print each procedure separately. It is faster to print all the procedures in the workbook at one time by clicking the Current Project option button to select it. You can also create a file of the VBA code by selecting the Print to File check box. You do not want to print the modules at this time.

6. **Click Cancel in the Print - VBAProject dialog box**

7. **Click the View Microsoft Excel button 🗗 on the toolbar**

8. **Save the EX P-January Sales 2 workbook, then preview the worksheet**

   Compare your formatted worksheet to **FIGURE P-18**.

9. **Close the EX P-January Sales 2 workbook, close the EX P-Monthly Sales workbook, then exit Excel**

Running a macro using a button

You can run a macro by assigning it to a button on your worksheet. Create a button by clicking the Insert tab, clicking the Shapes button in the Illustrations group, choosing a shape, then drawing the shape on the worksheet. After you create the button, right-click it, click Assign Macro, then click the macro the button will run and click OK. It is a good idea to label the button with descriptive text; select it and begin typing. You can also format macro buttons using clip art, photographs, fills, and shadows. You format a button using the buttons on the DRAWING TOOLS FORMAT tab. To add a fill to the button, click the Shape Fill list arrow and select a fill color,

picture, texture, or gradient. To add a shape effect, click the Shape Effects button and select an effect. You can also use the WordArt styles in the WordArt Styles group. **FIGURE P-15** shows a button formatted with a gradient, bevel and WordArt.

FIGURE P-15: Formatted macro button

FIGURE P-16: Result of running MainProcedure procedure

Formatted title

Row inserted

Total sales calculated

Sales status message inserted

FIGURE P-17: Printing options for macro procedures

Current Project option button

Print to File check box

FIGURE P-18: Formatted January worksheet

Quest Chicago January Sales

Trip Code	Depart Date	Number of Days	Seats Sold	Tour	Sales
457R	1/7/2016	30	30	African National Parks	$ 121,400.00
556J	1/13/2016	14	25	Amazing Amazon	$ 67,875.00
675Y	1/19/2016	14	32	Catalonia Adventure	$ 100,300.00
446R	1/20/2016	7	18	Yellowstone	$ 46,958.00
251D	1/21/2016	7	10	Costa Rica	$ 28,220.00
335P	1/22/2016	21	33	Corfu Sailing Voyage	$ 105,270.00
431V	1/25/2016	7	21	Costa Rica Rainforests	$ 54,390.00
215C	1/26/2016	14	19	Silk Road Travels	$ 92,663.00
325B	1/27/2016	10	17	Down Under Exodus	$ 47,600.00
311A	1/29/2016	18	20	Essential India	$ 102,887.00
422R	1/29/2016	7	24	Exotic Morocco	$ 45,600.00
331E	1/30/2016	12	21	Experience Cambodia	$ 98,557.00
831P	1/30/2016	14	15	Galapagos Adventure	$ 55,698.00
337Q	1/31/2016	18	10	Green Adventures in Ecuador	$ 39,574.00
				Monthly Total:	$ 1,006,992.00
				Sales Status:	Met Quota

Your Name   11/30/2016

Excel 2013

Practice

Concepts Review

1. **Which element do you click to return to Excel from the Visual Basic Editor?**
2. **Which element points to the Project Explorer window?**
3. **Which element points to the Code window?**
4. **Which element do you click to turn off the Step Into feature?**
5. **Which element points to comments in the VBA code?**

FIGURE P-19

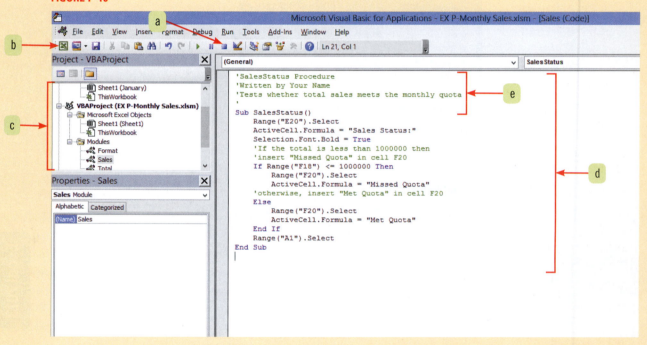

Match each term with the statement that best describes it.

6. **Sub procedure**
7. **Function**
8. **Keywords**
9. **Procedure**
10. **Comments**

a. Another term for a macro in Visual Basic for Applications (VBA)
b. A procedure that returns a value
c. Words that are recognized as part of the programming language
d. A series of statements that perform an action but don't return a value
e. Descriptive text used to explain parts of a procedure

Select the best answer from the list of choices.

11. **A location in memory where you can temporarily store information is a:**
    a. Variable.
    b. Procedure.
    c. Sub procedure.
    d. Function.

12. **You enter the statements of a macro in:**
    a. The Macro dialog box.
    b. Any blank worksheet.
    c. The Properties window of the Visual Basic Editor.
    d. The Code window of the Visual Basic Editor.

13. **If your macro doesn't run correctly, you should:**
    a. Select the macro in the Macro dialog box, click Step Into, then debug the macro.
    b. Create an If...Then...Else statement.
    c. Click the Project Explorer button.
    d. Click the Properties button.

14. **Comments are displayed in _____ in VBA code.**
    a. Black
    b. Blue
    c. Red
    d. Green

15. **Keywords are displayed in _____ in VBA code.**
    a. Black
    b. Blue
    c. Green
    d. Red

Skills Review

1. **View and analyze VBA code.**
   a. Start Excel, open the file EX P-3.xlsm from the location where you store your Data Files, enable macros, then save it as **EX P-Home Products**.
   b. Review the unformatted December worksheet.
   c. Open the Visual Basic Editor.
   d. Select the DataFormat module, and review the Format procedure.
   e. Insert comments in the procedure code describing what action you think each line of code will perform. (*Hint*: One of the statements will sort the list by Store #.) Add comment lines to the top of the procedure to describe the purpose of the macro and to enter your name.
   f. Save the macro, return to the worksheet, then run the Format macro.
   g. Compare the results with the code and your comments.
   h. Save the workbook.

2. **Write VBA code.**
   a. Open the Visual Basic Editor, and insert a new module named **Total** in the EX P-Home Products project.
   b. Enter the code for the SalesTotal procedure exactly as shown in **FIGURE P-20**. Enter your name in the second line.
   c. Save the macro.
   d. Return to the December worksheet, then run the SalesTotal macro.
   e. Save the workbook.

FIGURE P-20

```
'SalesTotal Procedure
'Written by Your Name
'Totals December sales
Sub SalesTotal()
    Range("E17").Select
    ActiveCell.Formula = "=SUM($E$3:$E$16)"
    Selection.Font.Bold = True
    With Selection.Borders(xlTop)
        .LineStyle = xlSingle
    End With
    Columns("E").Select
    Selection.Columns.AutoFit
    Range("A1").Select
End Sub
```

Skills Review (continued)

3. Add a conditional statement

a. Open the Visual Basic Editor, and insert a new module named **Goal** in the EX P-Home Products project.

b. Enter the SalesGoal procedure exactly as shown in **FIGURE P-21**. Enter your name on the second line.

c. Save the macro.

d. Return to the December worksheet, and run the SalesGoal macro. The procedure should enter the message **Missed goal** in cell E18. Save the workbook.

FIGURE P-21

```
'SalesGoal Procedure
'Written by Your Name
'Tests whether sales goal was met
Sub SalesGoal()
    'If the total is >=100000, then insert "Met Goal"
    'in cell E18
    If Range("E17") >= 100000 Then
        Range("E18").Select
        ActiveCell.Formula = "Met goal"
    'otherwise, insert "Missed goal" in cell E18
    Else
        Range("E18").Select
        ActiveCell.Formula = "Missed goal"
    End If
    Range("A1").Select
End Sub
```

4. Prompt the user for data.

a. Open the Visual Basic Editor, and insert a new module named **Header** in the EX P-Home Products project.

b. Enter the HeaderFooter procedure exactly as shown in **FIGURE P-22**. You are entering an error in the procedure that will be corrected in Step 5.

c. Save the macro, then return to the December worksheet, and run the HeaderFooter macro.

d. Preview the December worksheet. Your name should be missing from the left section of the footer.

e. Save the workbook.

FIGURE P-22

```
'HeaderFooter Procedure
'Written by Your Name
'Procedure to customize the header and footer
Sub HeaderFooter()
    'Inserts the filename in the header
    Worksheets("December").PageSetup.CenterHeader = "&F"
    'Declares the variable LeftFooterText as a string
    Dim LeftFooterText As String
    'Prompts user for left footer text
    LeftFooter = InputBox("Enter your full name:")
    'Inserts response into left footer
    Worksheets("December").PageSetup.LeftFooter = LeftFooterText
    'Inserts the date into right footer
    Worksheets("December").PageSetup.RightFooter = "&D"
End Sub
```

5. Debug a macro.

a. Return to the Visual Basic Editor and use the Step Into feature to locate where the error occurred in the HeaderFooter procedure. Use the Reset button to turn off the debugger.

b. Edit the procedure in the Visual Basic Editor to correct the error. (*Hint*: The error occurs on the line: LeftFooter = InputBox("Enter your full name:"). The variable that will input the response text into the worksheet footer is LeftFooterText. The line should be: LeftFooterText = InputBox("Enter your full name:").)

c. Save the macro, then return to the December worksheet, and run the HeaderFooter macro again.

d. Verify that your name now appears in the left section of the footer, then save the file.

6. Create and run a main procedure.

a. Return to the Visual Basic Editor, insert a new module, then name it **MainProc**.

b. Begin the main procedure by entering comments in the code window that provide the procedure's name (MainProcedure) and explain that its purpose is to run the Format, SalesTotal, SalesGoal, and HeaderFooter procedures. Enter your name in a comment.

c. Enter the procedure header **Sub MainProcedure()**.

d. Enter four Call statements that will run the Format, SalesTotal, SalesGoal, and HeaderFooter procedures in sequence.

e. Save the procedure and return to Excel.

f. Open the file EX P-3.xlsm, then save it as **EX P-Home Products 2**.

g. Run the MainProcedure macro, entering your name when prompted. (*Hint*: In the Macro dialog box, the macro procedures you created will now have EX P-Home Products.xlsm! as part of their names. This is because the macros are stored in the EX P-Home Products workbook, not in the EX P-Home Products 2 workbook.)

Skills Review (continued)

h. Verify that the macro ran successfully by comparing your worksheet to **FIGURE P-23**.

i. Save the EX P-Home Products 2 workbook, preview the December worksheet to check the header and footer, then close the EX P-Home Products 2 workbook.

j. Save the EX P-Home Products workbook, close the workbook, exit Excel, then submit the EX P-Home Products workbook to your instructor.

FIGURE P-23

	A	B	C	D	E
1	Home Products December Sales				
2	Store #	City	State	Manager	Sales
3	11405	Juno	FL	Clifford	$ 8,645.93
4	19404	Palm Beach	FL	Cloutier	$ 8,656.83
5	29393	Tampa	FL	Nelson	$ 7,654.32
6	29396	Cape Coral	FL	Enos	$ 9,583.66
7	29399	Daytona	FL	DiBenedetto	$ 9,228.33
8	29402	Vero Beach	FL	Guapo	$ 5,534.34
9	29406	Miami	FL	Monroe	$ 4,987.36
10	39394	Naples	FL	Hamm	$ 6,715.68
11	39395	Bonita Springs	FL	Handelmann	$ 4,225.22
12	39397	Clearwater	FL	Erickson	$ 7,594.22
13	39398	Delray Beach	FL	Dever	$ 8,442.90
14	39400	Stuart	FL	Hahn	$ 8,001.34
15	39401	Neptune	FL	Pratt	$ 5,251.22
16	39403	Sanibel	FL	Lo	$ 4,643.93
17					$99,165.28
18					Missed goal
19					

Independent Challenge 1

You are the development director at a private school. The information systems manager asks you to document and test an Excel procedure that the previous director wrote for the school's accountant. You will first run the macro procedure to see what it does, then add comments to the VBA code to document it. You will also enter data to verify that the formulas in the macro work correctly.

a. Start Excel, open the file EX P-4.xlsm from the location where you store your Data Files, then save it as **EX P-First Quarter**.

b. Run the First macro, noting anything that you think should be mentioned in your documentation.

c. Review the First procedure in the Visual Basic Editor. It is stored in the FirstQtr module.

d. Document the procedure by adding comments to the code, indicating the actions the procedure performs and the objects (ranges) that are affected.

e. Enter your name in a comment line, then save the procedure.

f. Return to the Jan-Mar worksheet, and use **FIGURE P-24** as a guide to enter data in cells B4:D6. The totals will appear as you enter the income data.

g. Format the range B4:D8 using the Accounting Number format with no decimals, as shown in **FIGURE P-24**.

h. Check the total income calculations in row 8 to verify that the macro is working correctly.

i. Enter your name in the center section of the Jan-Mar sheet footer, save the workbook, then preview the worksheet.

j. Close the workbook, exit Excel, then submit the workbook to your instructor.

FIGURE P-24

	A	B	C	D	E
1		January	February	March	
2	Income				
3					
4	Donations	$ 1,700	$ 1,700	$ 1,500	
5	Fundraisers	$ 3,000	$ 2,100	$ 2,700	
6	Grants	$ 21,000	$ 51,000	$ 92,000	
7					
8	Total Income	$ 25,700	$ 54,800	$ 96,200	
9					

Independent Challenge 2

You work in the Miami branch of Medical Resources, a medical employment recruitment agency. You have three locations where you have monthly quotas for placements. Each month you are required to produce a report stating whether placement quotas were met for the following three medical facilities: Central Hospital, Shore Clinic, and Assisted Home. The quotas for each month are as follows: Central Hospital 12, Shore Clinic 8, and Assisted Home 5. Your placement results this month were 8, 9, and 6, respectively. You decide to create a procedure to automate your monthly task of determining the placement quota status for the placement categories. You would like your assistant to take this task over when you go on vacation next month. Because he has no previous experience with Excel, you decide to create a second procedure that prompts a user with input boxes to enter the actual placement results for the month.

a. Start Excel, open the file EX P-5.xlsm from the location where you store your Data Files, then save it as **EX P-Placements**.

Excel 2013

Independent Challenge 2 (continued)

b. Use the Visual Basic Editor to insert a new module named **Quotas** in the EX P-Placements workbook. Create a procedure in the new module named **PlacementQuota** that determines the quota status for each category and enters Yes or No in the Status column. The VBA code is shown in **FIGURE P-25**.

c. Add comments to the PlacementQuota procedure, including the procedure name, your name, and the purpose of the procedure, then save it.

d. Insert a new module named **MonthlyPlacement**. Create a second procedure named **Placement** that prompts a user for placement data for each placement category, enters the input data in the appropriate cells, then calls the PlacementQuota procedure. The VBA code is shown in **FIGURE P-26**. (*Hint*: The procedure's blank lines group the macro code in related units. These blank lines are optional and their purpose is to make the procedure easier to understand.)

e. Add a comment noting the procedure name on the first line. Add a comment with your name on the second line. Add a third comment line at the top of the procedure describing its purpose. Enter comments in the code to document the macro actions. Save the procedure.

f. Run the Placement macro, and enter **8** for hospital placement, **9** for clinic placements, and **6** for assisted placements. Correct any errors in the VBA code.

g. Add your name to the center section of the worksheet footer, save the workbook, then preview the worksheet. Close the workbook, exit Excel, then submit your workbook to your instructor.

FIGURE P-25

```
Sub PlacementQuota()

    If Range("C4") >= 12 Then
        Range("D4").Select
        ActiveCell.Formula = "Yes"
    Else
        Range("D4").Select
        ActiveCell.Formula = "No"
    End If

    If Range("C5") >= 8 Then
        Range("D5").Select
        ActiveCell.Formula = "Yes"
    Else
        Range("D5").Select
        ActiveCell.Formula = "No"
    End If

    If Range("C6") >= 5 Then
        Range("D6").Select
        ActiveCell.Formula = "Yes"
    Else
        Range("D6").Select
        ActiveCell.Formula = "No"
    End If

End Sub
```

FIGURE P-26

```
Sub Placement()

    Dim Hospital As String
    Hospital = InputBox("Enter Hospital Placements")
    Range("C4").Select
    Selection = Hospital

    Dim Clinic As String
    Clinic = InputBox("Enter Clinic Placements")
    Range("C5").Select
    Selection = Clinic

    Dim Assisted As String
    Assisted = InputBox("Enter Assisted Placements")
    Range("C6").Select
    Selection = Assisted

    Call PlacementQuota

End Sub
```

Independent Challenge 3

You are the marketing director at a car dealership business based in Cincinnati. You have started to advertise using an area magazine, billboards, TV, radio, and local newspapers. Every month you prepare a report with the advertising expenses detailed by source. You decide to create a macro that will format the monthly reports. You add the same footers on every report, so you will create another macro that will add a footer to a document. Finally, you will create a main procedure that calls the macros to format the report and adds a footer. You begin by opening a workbook with the January data. You will save the macros you create in this workbook.

a. Start Excel, open the file EX P-6.xlsm from the location where you store your Data Files, then save it as **EX P-Auto**.

b. Insert a module named **Format**, then create a procedure named **Formatting** that:

- Selects a cell in row 3, and inserts a row in the worksheet above it.
- Selects the cost data in column C, and formats it as currency. (*Hint*: After the row is inserted, this range is C5:C9.)
- Selects cell A1 before ending.

c. Save the Formatting procedure.

d. Insert a module named **Foot**, then create a procedure named **Footer** that:

- Declares a string variable for text that will be placed in the left footer.
- Uses an input box to prompt the user for his or her name, and places the name in the left footer.
- Places the date in the right footer.

Independent Challenge 3 (continued)

e. Save the Footer procedure.

f. Insert a module named **Main**, then create a procedure named **MainProc** that calls the Footer procedure and the Formatting procedure.

g. Save your work, then run the MainProc procedure. Debug each procedure as necessary. Your worksheet should look like **FIGURE P-27**.

h. Document each procedure by inserting a comment line with the procedure name, your name, and a description of the procedure.

i. Preview the January worksheet, save the workbook, close the workbook, exit Excel, then submit the workbook to your instructor.

FIGURE P-27

A	B	C	D
1	Cincinnati Auto		
2	Ad Campaign		
3			
Advertising Type	**Source**	**Cost**	
Magazine	Ohio Magazine	$ 350.00	
Newspaper	Tribune	$ 150.00	
Billboard	Main Street	$ 450.00	
TV	Local Access Station	$ 170.00	
Radio	WAQV	$ 575.00	

Independent Challenge 4: Explore

You decide to create a log of your monthly expenses in an effort to budget your income. You have received a workbook with a macro that tracks your major expenses for the first three months of the year. You want to expand this macro to track six months of expenses.

a. Start Excel, open the file EX P-7.xlsm from the location where you store your Data Files, then save it as **EX P-Expenses**.

b. Run the MonthExpenses macro and enter expense numbers to verify the macro is working properly, then clear all the expense entries in cells E2:E7.

c. Edit the MonthExpenses procedure to add the abbreviated month entries of Apr, May, and Jun. Remember to edit the selected cells, total cells and the formatting ranges in the procedure.

d. Run the macro and debug the procedure as necessary. Enter expense numbers to verify the macro is working properly. Widen columns where necessary.

e. Save your work.

f. Verify that the totals are correct for each month and each category.

g. Enter your name as a comment in the second line of the procedure, then save the procedure.

h. Change the page orientation to landscape, enter your name in the center section of the worksheet footer, then preview the worksheet.

i. Insert a module named **Preview** with a procedure named **PreviewSheetdata** that previews a worksheet. The VBA code is shown in **FIGURE P-28**.

j. Save the macro and return to the worksheet.

k. Assign the macro PreviewSheetdata to a button on the worksheet. (*Hint*: Use the Rectangle tool to create the button, label the button **Print Preview**, then right-click the button to assign the macro.)

l. Format the button and its label with a style of your choice.

m. Test the button, then close the Print Preview.

n. Save the workbook, close the workbook, exit Excel, then submit the workbook to your instructor.

FIGURE P-28

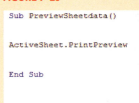

```
Sub PreviewSheetdata()

ActiveSheet.PrintPreview

End Sub
```

Excel 2013

Visual Workshop

Open the file EX P-8.xlsm from the location where you store your Data Files, then save it as **EX P-Florist**. Create a macro procedure named **Formatting** in a module named **FormatFile** that will format the worksheet as shown in FIGURE P-29. (*Hints*: The font size of the first two rows is 12 pt and the other rows are 11 pt. Notice that there is an added row.) Run the macro and debug it as necessary to make the worksheet match FIGURE P-29. Insert your name in a comment line under the procedure name and in the worksheet footer, then preview the worksheet. Submit the workbook to your instructor.

FIGURE P-29

	A	B	C
1	Blossoms		
2	Monthly Sales		
3			
4	Flowers	$857.89	
5	Plants	$622.87	
6	Silks	$424.58	
7	Home Décor	$469.88	
8			
9			

Glossary

Apply (a template) To open a document based on an Excel template.

Argument In the Visual Basic for Applications (VBA) programming language, variable used in procedures that a main procedure might run. *See also* Main procedure.

ASCII file A text file that contains data but no formatting; instead of being divided into columns, ASCII file data are separated, or delimited, by tabs or commas.

Attributes Styling characteristics such as bold, italic, and underlining that you can apply to change the way text and numbers look in a worksheet or chart. In XML, the components that provide information about the document's elements.

Auditing An Excel feature that helps track errors and check worksheet logic.

AutoComplete In the Visual Basic for Applications (VBA) programming language, a list of words that appears as you enter code; helps you automatically enter elements with the correct syntax.

Bug In programming, an error that causes a procedure to run incorrectly.

Call statement A Visual Basic statement that retrieves a procedure that you want to run, using the syntax Call *procedurename*.

Category axis Horizontal axis of a chart, usually containing the names of data groups; in a 2-dimensional chart, also known as the x-axis.

Cell comments Notes you've written about a workbook that appear when you place the pointer over a cell.

Change history A worksheet containing a list of changes made to a shared workbook.

Code *See* Program code.

Code window In the Visual Basic Editor, the window that displays the selected module's procedures, written in the Visual Basic programming language.

Combination chart A chart that combines two or more chart types in a single chart.

Compatible The capability of different programs to work together and exchange data.

Custom chart type A specially formatted Excel chart.

Data source Worksheet data used to create a chart or a PivotTable.

Data validation A feature that allows you to specify what data is allowable (valid) for a range of cells.

Database An organized collection of related information. In Excel, a database is called a table.

Database program An application, such as Microsoft Access, that lets you manage large amounts of data organized in tables.

Database table A set of data organized using columns and rows that is created in a database program.

Debug In programming, to find and correct an error in code.

Declare In the Visual Basic programming language, to assign a type, such as numeric or text, to a variable.

Delimiter A separator such as a space, comma, or semicolon between elements in imported data.

Destination program In a data exchange, the program that will receive the data.

Document To make notes about basic worksheet assumptions, complex formulas, or questionable data. In a macro, to insert comments that explain the Visual Basic code.

Edit Link A link to a workbook on a SkyDrive that can be edited by users.

Element An XML component that defines the document content.

Embed To insert a copy of data into a destination document; you can double-click the embedded object to modify it using the tools of the source program.

Embedded chart A chart displayed as an object in a worksheet.

Encrypted data Data protected by use of a password, which encodes it in a form that only authorized people with a password can decode.

Extensible Markup Language (XML) A system for defining languages using tags to structure data.

Field In a table (an Excel database) or PivotTable, a column that describes a characteristic about records, such as first name or city. In a PivotTable, drag field names to PivotTable row, column, data, or report filter areas to explore data relationships.

Form control An object that can be added to a worksheet to help users enter data. An example is a list box form control.

Function (Excel) A built-in formula that includes the information necessary to calculate an answer; for example, SUM (for calculating a sum) or FV (for calculating the future value of an investment) (Visual Basic) In the Visual Basic for Applications (VBA) programming language, a predefined procedure that returns a value, such as the InputBox function that prompts the user to enter information.

Goal cell In backsolving, a cell containing a formula in which you can substitute values to find a specific value, or goal.

If...Then...Else statement In the Visual Basic programming language, a conditional statement that directs Excel to perform specified actions under certain conditions; its syntax is "If *condition* Then *statements* Else [*elsestatements*]".

Integration A process in which data is exchanged among Excel and other Windows programs; can include pasting, importing, exporting, embedding, and linking.

Keyword (Excel) Terms added to a workbook's Document Properties that help locate the file in a search. (Macros) In a macro procedure, a word that is recognized as part of the Visual Basic programming language.

Linear trendline In an Excel chart, a straight line representing an overall trend in a data series.

Link To insert an object into a destination program; the information you insert will be updated automatically when the data in the source document changes.

Main procedure A macro procedure containing several macros that run sequentially.

Manual calculation An option that turns off automatic calculation of worksheet formulas, allowing you to selectively determine if and when you want Excel to perform calculations.

Map An XML schema that is attached to a workbook.

Map an XML element A process in which XML element names are placed on an Excel worksheet in specific locations.

Mode In dialog boxes, a state that offers a limited set of possible choices.

Modeless Describes dialog boxes that, when opened, allow you to select other elements on a chart or worksheet to change the dialog box options and format, or otherwise alter the selected elements.

Object A chart or graphic image that can be moved and resized and contains handles when selected. In object linking and embedding (OLE), the data to be exchanged between another document or program. In Visual Basic, every Excel element, including ranges.

Object Linking and Embedding (OLE) A Microsoft Windows technology that allows you to transfer data from one document and program to another using embedding or linking.

Office App Applications that can be added to a worksheet to help manage and personalize the data. Examples are maps, dictionaries, and calendars.

OLE *See* Object Linking and Embedding.

Outline symbols In outline view, the buttons that, when clicked, change the amount of detail in the outlined worksheet.

PivotChart report An Excel feature that lets you summarize worksheet data in the form of a chart in which you can rearrange, or "pivot," parts of the chart structure to explore new data relationships. Also called a PivotChart.

PivotTable Field List A window containing fields that can be used to create or modify a PivotTable.

PivotTable Report An Excel feature that allows you to summarize worksheet data in the form of a table in which you can rearrange, or "pivot," parts of the table structure to explore new data relationships; also called a PivotTable.

Plot area In a chart, the area inside the horizontal and vertical axes.

Populate The process of importing an XML file and filling the mapped elements on the worksheet with data from the XML file. Also the process of adding data or fields to a table, PivotTable, or a worksheet.

Presentation graphics program A program such as Microsoft PowerPoint that you can use to create slide show presentations.

Primary key The field in a database that contains unique information for each record.

Procedure A sequence of Visual Basic statements contained in a macro that accomplishes a specific task.

Procedure footer In Visual Basic, the last line of a Sub procedure.

Procedure header The first line in a Visual Basic procedure, it defines the procedure type, name, and arguments.

Project In the Visual Basic Editor, the equivalent of a workbook; a project contains Visual Basic modules.

Project Explorer In the Visual Basic Editor, a window that lists all open projects (or workbooks) and the worksheets and modules they contain.

Properties window In the Visual Basic Editor, the window that displays a list of characteristics, or properties, associated with a module.

Property In Visual Basic, an attribute of an object that describes its character or behavior.

Range object In Visual Basic, an object that represents a cell or a range of cells.

Refresh To update a PivotTable so it reflects changes to the underlying data.

Regression analysis A way of representing data with a mathematically-calculated trendline showing the overall trend represented by the data.

Report filter A feature that allows you to specify the ranges you want summarized in a PivotTable.

Schema In an XML document, a list of the fields, called elements or attributes, and their characteristics.

Share *See* Shared workbook.

Shared workbook An Excel workbook that several users can open and modify.

Slicer A graphic object used to filter a PivotTable.

SmartArt graphic Predesigned diagram types for the following types of data: List, Process, Cycle, Hierarchy, Relationship, Matrix, and Pyramid.

Source program In a data exchange, the program used to create the data you are embedding or linking.

Statement In Visual Basic, a line of code.

Strong password A password that is difficult to guess and that helps to protect your workbooks from security threats; has at least 14 characters that are a mix of upper- and lowercase letters, numbers, and special characters.

Sub procedure A series of Visual Basic statements that performs an action but does not return a value.

Summary function In a PivotTable, a function that determines the type of calculation applied to the PivotTable data, such as SUM or COUNT.

Syntax In the Visual Basic programming language, the formatting rules that must be followed so that the macro will run correctly.

Template A file whose content or formatting serves as the basis for a new workbook; Excel template files have the file extension . xltx. the macro will run correctly.

Text file *See* ASCII file.

Toggle A button with two settings, on and off.

Tracer arrows In Excel worksheet auditing, arrows that point from cells that might have caused an error to the active cell containing an error.

Track To identify and keep a record of who makes which changes to a workbook.

Username The name that appears in the User name text box of the Excel Options dialog box. This name is displayed at the beginning of comments added to a worksheet.

Validate A process in which an XML schema makes sure the XML data follows the rules outlined in the schema.

Validation *See* Data Validation.

Value axis In a chart, vertical axis that contains numerical values; in a 2-dimensional chart, also known as the y-axis.

VBA *See* Visual Basic for Applications.

View Link A link to a workbook on a SkyDrive that can be viewed by users.

Web query An Excel feature that lets you obtain data from a Web, Internet, or intranet site and places it in an Excel workbook for analysis.

What-if analysis A decision-making tool in which data is changed and formulas are recalculated in order to predict various possible outcomes.

Write access The ability to make changes to a workbook; with read access, a user can only read the workbook contents and cannot make changes.

XML (Extensible Markup Language) A system for defining languages using tags to structure, store, and send data.

Index